THE FRENCH FARMHOUSE KITCHEN

THE FRENCH FARMHOUSE KITCHEN

Eileen Reece

Exeter Books

NEW YORK

Cover: *Filet de porc en venaison. Courgettes à la sauge.*

First published in USA 1984
by Exeter Books
Distributed by Bookthrift
Exeter is a registered trademark of Simon & Schuster, Inc.
Bookthrift is a registered trademark of Simon & Schuster, Inc.
New York, New York.

ISBN 0-671-06542-4

Printed in Hong Kong

Contents

WEIGHTS AND MEASURES

Imperial	US
2½ oz Allbran	1 cup
1 lb apples (diced)	4 cups
2 oz bacon, streaky	3 slices fatty bacon
2 oz bean sprouts	1 cup
4 oz black or redcurrants, blueberries	1 cup
4 oz breadcrumbs (fine dried)	1 cup
2 oz breadcrumbs (fresh soft), cake crumbs	1 cup
8 oz butter, margarine, lard, dripping	1 cup butter, margarine, shortening, drippings
3-4 oz button mushrooms	1 cup
8 oz cabbage (finely chopped)	3 cups
12 oz clear honey, golden syrup, molasses, black treacle	1 cup (1 lb =1⅓ cups) honey, maple syrup, molasses, black treacle
1 oz cooking chocolate	1 square baking chocolate
4½ oz cornflour	1 cup cornstarch
8 oz cottage, cream cheese	1 cup
¼ pint single, double cream	½ cup + 2 tablespoons (⅔ cup) light, heavy cream
2 oz curry powder	½ cup
3 oz desiccated coconut	1 cup shredded coconut
4 oz digestive biscuits (8 biscuits)	1 cup Graham crackers
7 oz dried chick peas, haricot beans	1 cup garbanzos, navy beans
4 oz flour, plain or self-raising	2 tablespoons all-purpose or self-rising flour
½ oz gelatine (1 tablespoon sets 2 cups liquid)	2 envelopes
3 oz preserved ginger (chopped)	⅓ cup
8 oz glacé cherries	1 cup candied cherries
3½ lbs gooseberries	9 cups
4 oz grated cheese, Cheddar type, Parmesan	1 cup
4 oz ground almonds	1 cup
7 oz long-grain rice	1 cup
4 oz macaroni, raw	1 cup
8 oz mashed potato	1 cup
8 oz minced raw meat	1 cup ground raw meat, firmly packed
4 oz nuts (chopped)	1 cup
2 oz onion (chopped)	½ cup
2 oz parsley (chopped)	1½ cups
6 oz pickled beetroot (chopped)	1 cup
6 oz peeled prawns	1 cup peeled shrimp
5-6 oz raisins, currants, sultanas (chopped), candied peel	1 cup (1 lb =3 cups)
5 oz raspberries	1 cup
3½ oz rolled oats	1 cup
8 oz sausagemeat	1 cup
5 oz strawberries, whole	1 cup
8 oz sugar, castor or granulated	1 cup, firmly packed
4 oz sugar, icing (sieved)	1 cup sifted confectioner's sugar
8 oz tomatoes (chopped)	1 cup
2¾ oz (smallest can) tomato purée	¼ cup
4 teaspoons dried yeast	4 teaspoons active dry yeast
¼ pint yoghurt	½ cup + 2 tablespoons (⅔ cup)

Liquid Measurements

20 fluid oz =1 Imperial pint	16 fluid oz =1 American pint
10 fluid oz =½ Imperial pint	8 fluid oz =1 American cup

Introduction

The French farm kitchen in no way resembles its English equivalent. The farmhouse itself, issue of bitter bloodshed when land was wrenched from aristocratic possession by an exploited peasantry in the Revolution of 1789, has no gracious atmosphere. The hard driving force that acquired it still exists in running it.

The farm is, for each family, a small industry in which all its members work, male and female alike, striving side by side to enrich and enlarge the holding so hard won by their ancestors.

In Lorraine, however, and in the more remote parts of the country, beautiful farmhouses which escaped the holocaust of the Revolution still exist. But the average French farmhouse has none of the architectural beauty for which so many of our own are noted. The present trend for interior decoration has passed them by, although the one room in the house that is likely to have been improved is the kitchen. The hard-working French farmer's main concern is food, growing it, raising it and eating it. In an economy where young and old work in the fields in order to reduce expenditure to a minimum, the only money parted with willingly is for food.

Like most farmers the world over their main diet consists of home produce: vegetables, eggs, milk, rabbits and pork with occasional treats of poultry and game in season. But the French farmer's wife also buys butcher's meat, fish, cheeses and fruit throughout the year. This, however, does not diminish her almost obsessive sense of economy which allows no waste whatsoever.

At the same time her culinary standards are high, and with the rational mind of her race, she knows that good food is essential to good work output. Moreover, she takes into account the fact that food is the Frenchman's daily pleasure, and one that never palls.

In addition to her high standards, the Frenchwoman has at her disposal an abundance of raw materials that is unrivalled by any country in the world thanks to the great variety of regional climates of France. Her repertory of good economical dishes is also unrivalled.

The recipes she uses are those used by her mother and grandmother before her. But while the everyday dishes are mainly of the type that can be prepared early and left to cook by themselves while she goes about her work on the farm, on Sundays and fête days more elaborate dishes are prepared. *Pâté* or some other appetising first course is added to the menu and a fruit tart will be served instead of fresh fruit.

But given any family event to celebrate, the humblest farm kitchen excels itself in the preparation of a gargantuan meal. Every village has its expert amateur cook for these occasions, and the country women called in 'to do the wedding' produce some of the best cooking in France.

Plans for the feast are laid weeks in advance and, with the expert presiding, the women of the family spend more time discussing the menu than they do discussing their clothes.

Delicacies of intricate preparation are proposed, one delectable dish after another is suggested and on the great day the culinary talent displayed has to be savoured to be believed.

The abundance of national produce, the Frenchman's discriminating palate, his wife's love of cooking and the country's instinctive appreciation of good living all contribute to a gastronomic standard that has won worldwide approval.

7

Kitchen Utensils

The French method of cooking the majority of their dishes in enamelled, cast-iron *cocottes* and casseroles, sealed with a heavy lid, is greatly responsible for the fine flavour of their food.

Since these utensils give the best results when used over the lowest possible heat the saving of fuel is considerable. But even more important to the cook, they preserve the most delicate flavours.

Ingredients cook in their own juices thanks to the thickness and weight of the pan. Vegetables cooked without water become a feast in themselves. The use of a Doufeu casserole with sunken lid which is filled with water to create condensation, produces meat remarkable for its tenderness, and its shrinkage during cooking is reduced to a minimum.

Pans such as these are found in every farm kitchen and in most cases have been handed down from one generation to the next. They are still made today exactly as they were first made in 1553 by Le Creuset at the Fonderies de Cousances.

The other type of pan without which no French kitchen is complete is the *sauteuse* which resembles a large straight-sided frying pan with a well fitting lid.

Not only is it invaluable when browning a considerable quantity of ingredients at once for casserole cooking, but a whole dish can be prepared and cooked in it. A jointed chicken, button onions and mushrooms are browned, a little wine and some herbs added, the lid firmly fixed in place and the *sauteuse* is then left for 1 . hours unattended. By this time a succulent dish with a good sauce is ready to be served, with the minimum of trouble and utensils involved. The professional version of the *sauteuse* is made of tin-lined copper, the domestic version of heavy cast-aluminium with a ground base which also assures even, steady, heat distribution.

Gratin dishes of cast-iron or ovenproof porcelain are important in French cooking. Their wide shallow form gives an extensive surface for the creation of the brown crust essential to many recipes. One very large and one family size are to be found in every kitchen from Boulogne to Bordeaux together with the popular *mouli-légumes*. This long established vegetable mill has not been ousted by the advent of the electric blender, perhaps because it costs so little in comparison.

Le Creuset utensils are sold in all kitchen equipment shops and kitchen sections of all large department stores throughout Europe and the United States. An illustrated brochure of the complete Le Creuset range can be obtained by post from: Clarbat Limited, 302 Barrington Road, London SW9 7JJ.

Copper *sauteuses*, *gratin* dishes, *mouli-légumes* from: David Mellor, 4 Sloane Square, London SW1W 8EE. Price list on request with s.a.e.

Heavy cast-aluminium *sauteuses* with lid from: Picquot Cook Ware, at all branches of Timothy Whites, larger branches of Boots, also The House of Fraser and kitchen equipment shops and department stores. Leaflet on request with s.a.e. from: Burrage and Boyde Ltd, Newmaid Works, Adnitt Road, Northampton NN1 5LD.

NOTES

It is important to follow **either** the metric **or** the imperial measures when using these recipes. All spoon measures are level.

Bread or breadcrumbs in all recipes should not be steam-baked. Oven-baked bread is easily obtained from small private bakeries.

8

Chapter One

HERBS,
SPICED SALTS
AND
FLAVOURED
VINEGARS

Herbs, use and cultivation

Fresh herbs are even more characteristic of French country cooking than are wine and cream, which are mainly used in regions where the climate favours their production, or in sophisticated urban dishes.

While the French farmer's wife has little time for tending flowers, apart from those that seed themselves around her kitchen door, she does grow culinary herbs in profusion and uses them constantly.

English cooks who have difficulty in obtaining them will find it easy to grow these essential herbs for themselves. Those who have no garden can grow most of them from seed indoors, and then transplant them into window boxes, or pots standing on a sunny window sill. Seeds and plants can be obtained from most garden centres.

The average well-drained garden soil will grow herbs successfully, and even difficult soils will give good results when compost, peat, hops or other humus-encouraging elements are added.

Difficult soils are a heavy clay soil which tends to become water-logged or, at the other end of the scale, a very light sandy soil which holds no moisture at all. There are a few herbs, however, that will flourish in almost any conditions, and these are mint, rosemary and thyme. The last two do require a sunny position. Once established, perennials will flourish indefinitely, especially if they are divided every three or four years.

Ideally, a herb garden should be surrounded by a low hedge of lavender or santolina to protect the plants from drying winds which rob them of their aroma.

Basil *Annual*
The young fresh leaves have a great affinity with all tomato dishes. They are an essential ingredient of *pestou* (see page 59) and are also used for flavouring veal, chicken and rabbit dishes.
Sow the seeds under glass in April, harden off and prick out the young plants in May. This herb also grows well in pots indoors and in window boxes, but needs hot sun in order to give full flavour. The leaves are best used fresh, not dried.

Bay *Perennial*
The dried or fresh leaves are used to flavour soups, casseroles, *pâtés* and some fruit dishes (e.g. baked pears).
The fresh leaves are very pungent, so use half the quantity advised for dried ones.
Cuttings of young wood are difficult to strike so it is best to buy the plant either as a shrub or a small tree. It will flourish in open ground or a wooden tub provided that it is protected from cold winds. The leaves are easily frost-bitten.

Bergamot *Perennial*
The leaves must be gathered before the plant flowers, and can be used dried to make an excellent *tisane* (see page 13).
The red, mauve or white flowers make a pleasing addition to the herbaceous border, where they flourish, preferably in a damp spot.
Buy the plant from a nursery gardener, or it can be divided early in spring. Bury the roots fairly deep, as they tend to work up to the surface and dry out.

Borage *Annual*
Use the fresh young leaves in salads. They give a cucumber-like flavour. Do not use mature leaves, as they are tough in texture.
Also used for making *tisane* and flavouring iced drinks and claret cup.
Sow seed in April and thin out when leaves form. Sown in late summer it will flower the following May.

Bouquet garni (1)
An ingredient indispensible in French cooking.
This little faggot of mixed herbs is quickly put together by cooks who grow their own herbs. It is used to flavour soups, sauces and many dishes of meat, fish or vegetables.

2 large stalks parsley
1 small sprig thyme and/or rosemary
1 bay leaf

Bouquet garni (2) (aromatique)
This more perfumed version of the *bouquet garni* is used for cooking bland meats like veal. Care must be taken in the amount of rosemary used as it has a very pungent flavour.

1 sprig winter or summer savory
1 small sprig rosemary
1 stalk tarragon
1 stalk chervil
1 stalk basil
1 large stalk celery

Chervil *Annual*
This is best used when fresh, in salads and with eggs and fish. It also makes an excellent summer soup (see page 22).
This herb, of the parsley family, is sown in the open from April/May onwards.
It bolts easily and once the flowers appear the plant is useless. Therefore, sow only a short row at a time, at intervals through the summer.

Chives *Perennial*
This short grass-like herb with a strong onion flavour is a great time-saver. Cut in a small bunch of about 15 to 20 strands and snipped up directly into the eggs for an omelette, a tomato or green salad or a sauce, it saves the trouble of peeling an onion.
Sow the seed outdoors in April or divide the clumps in spring or just after flowering in June.
It will flourish in a pot or a window box.

Corn salad *Biennial*
(Lamb's lettuce)
Can be treated as annual.
This is an excellent substitute for ordinary lettuce and grows much more quickly. In fact, it grows as fast as an annual herb, which is why it has been included in this list.
Sow outdoors in March to maintain a supply of salad throughout the summer, or sow in August and thin out to 20 cm (8 inches) apart to cut the round-leaved rosettes in early spring. A cloche or frame will encourage an early crop.

Dandelion *Perennial*
Dandelion, like corn salad, is grown as a commercial crop in France. The very young, tender rosettes of leaves make an excellent early spring salad (see page 63).
If the plant is grown for salad, the flower stalks must be removed as soon as they appear and the crowns must be blanched by covering them with an upturned flower pot. Where grown as a crop, the plants should be set out in a row, earthed up in autumn and covered with cloches or mulched with black polythene to produce tender early shoots in February.

Dill *Annual*
The dried seeds are used for flavouring vinegar and the soft feathery foliage for flavouring fish. This tall plant is an attractive addition to the herbaceous border.
Sow the seed in April or May in a drill and thin out the seedlings to 30 cm (12 inches) apart.

Fennel *Perennial*
A first cousin to dill in appearance, use and cultivation. An important ingredient of fish dishes, it has a distinctive aniseed flavour. Sweet fennel or Florence fennel is grown for the swollen stem joints which look like a slightly flattened, short head of celery. Fennel has few leaves and is used as a vegetable or raw in salad, and raw or dried as a flavouring. Propagation is from seed sown outdoors in April at 1.5 m (5 foot) intervals and thinned out to the strongest seedlings.

Garlic *Annual*

An aromatic much abused outside France. It is a flavouring and not a vegetable and, in consequence, must be used sparingly. A cut clove rubbed around the salad bowl and then discarded is sufficient to flavour a large salad, and two small cloves will flavour a large leg of lamb.

Grown from seed under glass the tiny bulbs are set out as soon as the ground is frost-free in April/May. Prick out to 15 cm (6 inches) apart, 7 cm (2½ inches) deep, in the sunniest place in the garden. The clusters of bulbs will be ripe in August and should be hung up in bunches in a dry, airy place until the skin and stems are quite dry and brittle.

Juniper *Perennial*

The berries are used in some *pâtés* and sauces and to flavour marinade for game. Juniper bushes with their blue-green foliage are very decorative, and can be bought from any nursery garden.

Marjoram *Annual & Perennial*

Both varieties are used for flavouring casseroles, *pâtés*, sauces and soups.

Sow sweet marjoram (annual) in a pot in March and place on a sunny window sill. Plant out in April/May, 30 cm (1 foot) apart in a sunny spot. Sow pot marjoram (perennial) in the same way or increase by root division. Plant in a warm position.

Mint *Perennial*

This herb is rarely used in French cooking. Mint sauce is unknown, but one of the most refreshing *tisanes* of all is made with the mint known as *Mentha piperata*. The leaves are darker than those of the ordinary variety. Any kind of mint, however, can be used for *tisane*.

A sprig of mint placed in a bottle of water will root quickly and will then grow profusely in any soil. In fact, it is advisable to restrict the roots by burying slates deeply around the plant to limit the space it should occupy.

Parsley *Biennial*

This herb is greatly used fresh, in sprigs, in a *bouquet garni*, or chopped and added to casseroles, omelettes and sauces. Also used in sprigs as a garnish, either fresh or fried.

Sow in a well drained soil in April/May when the soil has had time to warm up a little, or a spring crop can be obtained by sowing in August. To ensure rapid germination sow in a shallow drill and after covering with earth, moisten well with a kettleful of *boiling* water. If the leaves are covered with a cloche during bad weather, they can be cut throughout the winter. Remove the tall flowering stalk as soon as it appears.

This herb is not successful when dried: it loses its flavour quickly, often turning black and shrivelled when home-dried.

Rosemary *Perennial*

A popular herb in the French kitchen for composing a *bouquet garni* and for casseroles or dishes which need distinctive flavouring. It can be used fresh or dried, but beware of its pungent flavour and use it sparingly. A sprig of rosemary kept in a small bottle of olive oil, when brushed over lamb chops 1 hour before grilling, will flavour and tenderise them.

This decorative bush can be propagated by cuttings of non-flowering shoots taken in autumn and put into a cold frame or under a cloche for the winter, or cuttings can be taken in spring and placed in water until rooted.

A warm sunny site is necessary but this herb will grow quite well in a large pot.

Sage *Perennial*

Little used in French cooking and then only fresh, never dried, to flavour pork dishes and a few vegetable dishes.

The propagation is from summer cuttings taken with a heel. When planted out they require a sunny spot, but will flourish in any soil.

Savory *Annual & Perennial*
The flavour is very like that of thyme but somewhat sharper.

The leaves are used fresh in salads, sauces and stuffings.

Summer savory (annual) is sown in April and the leaves cut in summer, winter savory (perennial) is propagated by cuttings or division of roots in autumn or winter.

Shallots

An essential ingredient in French cooking, used for the distinctive flavour reminiscent of garlic. Used chopped in omelettes and stuffings.

When left whole, shallots are more presentable than onions in meat, poultry and game dishes. Also used in *pâtés* and for flavouring vinegar (see page 16).

Well cultivated, fairly heavily manured soil should be prepared and a top dressing of superphosphates given at planting time.

Bulbs are planted in March/April in drills 30 cm (1 foot) apart, 2.5 cm (1 inch) deep, with the soil pressed lightly around them, and the tip showing. They should not be pressed hard into the soil. When the bulbs split and swell and the green leaves turn yellow and die, lift bulbs and leave to dry on the ground in dry weather. If wet, place on boards and dry under cover. Store when ripe and firm, in one layer on a shelf in a cool airy shed. Reserve some firm bulbs for planting next season.

Sorrel *Perennial treated as annual*
(Sour grass)
This plant, very popular in French cooking, is part herb, part vegetable. It is used cooked as a vegetable, as flavouring, or raw in mixed salads. It is also used in omelettes and makes a delicious soup (see page 28).

Sow the seed in spring (April/May) in drills as for spinach and thin out to 20 cm (8 inches) apart when seedlings can be handled. All flower shoots should be picked out early as the plant bolts quickly.

Tarragon *Perennial*
Another essential herb in French cooking. It is used fresh to flavour salads, sauces, vegetable, fish and chicken dishes. It is also used to flavour vinegar (see page 16).

Sow the French variety (*Artemesia drancuculus*) in a pot indoors and plant out when the seedlings are sturdy enough to handle, in light sandy soil in a warm sheltered position with good drainage.

The plant can also be bought from a nurseryman or grown from cuttings or spring division. This herb keeps its flavour well when dried.

Thyme *Perennial*
Used in a *bouquet garni*, casseroles, sauces and stuffings. Should be used sparingly, the flavour is so pungent.

This herb dries well and is one of the very few which should be harvested when in flower, although only the nonflowering shoots are used. Propagation is effected by cuttings taken in spring and summer. They will flourish in very little soil providing it is alkaline and well drained, and a sunny position is provided.

Tisanes
Tisanes, or herb teas, are made by snipping up a large handful of fresh bergamot, borage or mint leaves and stalks into a jug and pouring 600 ml (1 pint) boiling water over them. Add a teaspoonful of sugar to draw out the flavour, cover and leave to infuse for a few minutes before serving. Mint tea especially is a very refreshing summer drink.

Drying and storing

Culinary herbs, when harvested for drying, should be cut on long stems in the early morning just after the dew has dried and before the sun is hot. Shake the leaves free of insects and spread the stems out on clean white paper with plenty of space between them. Place in a constantly heated airing cupboard or a dry airy loft out of direct light, so that the herbs will dry *slowly*.

Never dry them in sunlight or in a bathroom or kitchen where there is moisture in the air. Dry air, no direct light and an even temperature of about 32°C (90°F) are the necessary requirements.

Turn them over every other day so that they will dry evenly and as soon the stems are dry and brittle, pick off the leaves and rub them between the palms to an even consistency. Discard the stems.

Store the herbs in airtight containers but not in tins. Small screw-topped bottles lined with black paper to keep out the light are ideal. If no lining is used be sure to keep the bottles in a cupboard out of the light. Wooden boxes and drums make good containers too but, in either case, they should be small and airtight. Label each container with the name of the herb.

Fresh herbs can be deep-frozen but this process is not ideal. Some of them tend to become flaccid when so treated (e.g. parsley, bergamot, rosemary), and the flavour of most is impaired.

However, if large quantities are available, deep-freezing is worth a trial. Buy the waxed cardboard or plastic boxes sold for this purpose.

Cut the herbs when they are quite dry, but wash them free of grit and insects. Shake well and place a small quantity (enough to fill one container) in a colander, plunge it into a large pan of fast-boiling water for 1½ minutes. Drain and place immediately in the container. Seal and freeze at once.

Mixed herbs

The very special *herbes de Provence* (also called *herbes du Midi*), which can be bought at considerable expense in all kitchen equipment shops, are made at home in Provence where gardeners cultivate their herbs lovingly. This mixture is distinctive and gives a very special flavour to casseroled meat, game and fish.

Herbes de Provence

25 g (1 oz) each orange peel, dried bay leaves, garden thyme, wild thyme, savory, lavender, rosemary, cloves
1 nutmeg

Dry the orange peel in the bottom of the oven, when in use, until hard and brittle. When dry and cold, break into small pieces. Crumble the bay leaves and cut the nutmeg into chips with a sharp knife. Put all the ingredients into an electric grinder and grind to a medium-fine consistency. Store in dark glass bottles, or clear ones lined with black paper.

Spiced Salts

While salt cellars and pepper pots do appear on French dinner tables they are rarely used during the course of the meal. Gallic cooks can be deeply offended by guests who season their food at table. They believe in seasoning it correctly in the kitchen, during the cooking.

One preparation that country cooks use to great advantage is spiced and seasoned salt. It can take the place of a *bouquet garni* in quickly cooked dishes and allows the cook to concoct her own special mixture, varying the herbs to suit her family's taste. The following age-old recipe comes from a farm in Vendée.

Spiced Salt (1)

15 small dried bay leaves
225 g (8 oz) coarse sea salt crystals
1 nutmeg
7 g ($\frac{1}{4}$ oz) cloves
15 g ($\frac{1}{2}$ oz) white peppercorns
30 grains allspice
7 g ($\frac{1}{4}$ oz) dried marjoram
7 g ($\frac{1}{4}$ oz) dried thyme

Break up the bay leaves into pieces and grind them coarsely in an electric grinder. Pour them on to a sheet of white kitchen paper with the sea salt crystals and mix well. Cut the nutmeg into chips with a sharp knife, mix with the cloves, peppercorns and allspice and grind to the same consistency as the salt and bay leaves. Now mix in the marjoram and thyme and grind all ingredients together until they are the consistency of sand. Store in dark glass bottles and seal tightly, or line clear glass bottles with black paper before filling and sealing. The salt will keep indefinitely stored in this way.

Use 1 teaspoon spiced salt to 450 g (1 lb) dry ingredients or 1 litre (1$\frac{3}{4}$ pints) liquid.

A simpler but less subtle version of Spiced Salt can be made in the following way:

Spiced Salt (2)

160 g (5$\frac{1}{2}$ oz) peppercorns (white and black)
450 g (1 lb) coarse sea salt crystals
160 g (5$\frac{1}{2}$ oz) mixed spice

First grind the peppercorns to a medium texture resembling that of the salt crystals, then add the salt and grind them together finely. Spread on kitchen paper and blend in the mixed spice thoroughly. Store as in the previous recipe and use in the same quantity.

Flavoured Vinegars

Flavoured wine vinegar has been an important ingredient in French cooking since medieval times when vinegar was essential in order to keep meat edible in warm weather.

In the 13th century, street vendors were granted the right to cry their wares in the thoroughfares of Paris. These cries soon became famous, and the vinegar sellers even rolled their casks through the narrow streets crying 'Garlic and mustard vinegars, herb vinegar …' '*Vinaigres, bons et biaux.*'

They also sold *verjus*, the sieved juice of unripe grapes which serves to sharpen the flavour of many cooked dishes in the same way that vinegar does. It is still used in some country places and provides a means of using up green grapes unfit for any other purpose.

All farm kitchens have an earthenware vinegar barrel. It constitutes another of the many country economies. After the grape harvest, a certain quantity of either red or white wine is reserved and poured into the barrel over a liquid fungus or *mère de vinaigre* which turns it into vinegar. The quantity drawn off each day is replaced by emptying the remains of the wine bottles into the barrel.

When herbs are most pungent, just before flowering, they are cut and used to aromatise some of the vinegar drawn off. It is then bottled and used for flavouring.

Owning a vinegar barrel is a privilege of which few English kitchens can boast but plain wine vinegar sold in the multiple chemists' shops can be used effectively with home-grown herbs to produce fine vinegar at much less cost than that prepared commercially.

Flavoured Vinegar

For each 1 litre (1¾ pint) wine bottle allow:
1 litre (1¾ pints) plain wine vinegar
4 or 5 shallots, peeled and slightly crushed, threaded on fine string
or 4 cloves garlic, peeled and slightly crushed
or 2 tablespoons mustard seed
or 1 long leafy branch tarragon twice the length of the bottle

Collect the number of bottles necessary, with sound corks to fit. Wash the bottles in hot soapy water, rinse first in very hot water then in cold, drain, dry and heat in a slow oven. Scald the corks in boiling water.

Pour the vinegar into an enamel-lined or stainless steel pan and over a low temperature bring slowly to blood heat. It should be quite warm to the touch of a knuckle joint, no more. Add shallots, garlic, mustard seed or tarragon to the warm bottles. (If using tarragon, this should be bent double and pushed down the neck of the bottle.) Fill up with warm vinegar, cork down tightly, and place on a sunny window sill to mature for 6 weeks before use.

Opposite: A selection of fruit liqueurs, preserves, spices and flavoured oils and vinegars.
Overleaf: *Potée fraîche* (see page 32), *potage à l'oseille fermière* (see page 28).

16

Chapter Two

SOUPS

In French cooking, stock is made for use in sauces and casseroles. Soups are mostly prepared with water and the ingredients treated in a way that gives richness to the finished soup. The contents of French country soup-tureens are of infinite variety. While they mostly depend on the kitchen garden for their chief ingredients, the soup that the farm worker demands as his mainstay must be sustaining. Consequently, the farm cook has her own ways of introducing the ingredients which add nutritive value and body to the vegetable basis. She has three favourite methods of soup-making which are comprised in the following types of recipe.

1) *Pork and vegetable soups*
These soups are popular in all regions of France where every farm has a pig for domestic use. The belly of pork is cured at home by a very simple method (see page 83). This recipe will prove invaluable since pickled pork is used in the preparation of many French dishes. In soups it is mostly cooked in one piece or chopped very finely with some of the vegetable ingredients to provide savour and consistency, making in itself a complete and nourishing meal at relatively low cost.

2) *Vegetable soups*
The root vegetables, when prepared, are chopped, salted and cooked slowly with butter or poultry fat in a tightly sealed pan. This process makes the vegetables render their full flavour. Liquid is then added and the ingredients are simmered slowly to give a very savoury soup.

These hearty soups are served either with a piece of good butter stirred in, or with an egg yolk and cream or butter binding, or poured over slices of coarse farmhouse bread. In some cases the bread is made into crumbs which act as thickening.

3) *Meat broths*
These are made from reserved game and poultry bones and carcasses, which are first browned to enhance flavour and then simmered with herbs and vegetables to produce a fine quality broth.

Putting the carcass of a New Year's turkey or even the Sunday chicken to good use is an obligation for the French country cook. She collects the skin, carcass and other debris of any roast birds, the bones of hare and rabbit after *pâté* making, pieces of venison or other game not suitable for roasting and makes of it all a delectable broth. *La soupe du chasseur* uses all these otherwise wasted ingredients.

Soupe du chasseur
(Mixed Game Soup)
Serves 6–8

about 2 kg (4 lb) poultry and game bird carcasses and bones (skin and debris included)
3 litres (5 pints) water
1 tablespoon coarse sea salt
10 black peppercorns
4 juniper berries (lightly crushed)
¼ teaspoon cayenne pepper
1 large onion
2 cloves
2 leeks
2 large carrots
1 medium sized turnip
4 branches celery
4 stalks parsley
4 stalks chervil (optional)
1 sprig thyme
1 sprig marjoram
1 bay leaf
2 cloves garlic
1 stale French loaf

Break the carcasses and bones into small pieces. Spread them out in a large baking tin and brown them in the bottom of the oven when in use for other cooking. Put them into a large soup-pan with the skin and other debris and add water. Set over medium heat. As the froth rises remove it with a slotted spoon, and when boiling and cleared add salt, peppercorns, juniper and cayenne, reduce the heat to low and leave to simmer.

Meanwhile peel and trim the vegetables. Cut the onion into halves and stick a clove into each one. Cut the leeks into short lengths, green part included, slice the carrots thinly, quarter the turnip, and tie the celery and herbs into two small bundles.

Peel 1 clove of garlic and add to the pan together with the vegetables and herbs. Increase the heat slightly and when boiling point is reached again, lower it to minimum, cover the pan and leave to simmer for about 3 hours. The broth must simmer as slowly as possible to make the ingredients render their full savour.

Owners of Aga cookers can place the soup in the slow oven and leave it overnight.

In preparation for serving cut the bread into medium thin slices, rub with the remaining clove of garlic cut into halves, and put the bread in the oven or under a slow grill to bake dry and hard.

To serve, strain the contents of the soup-pan through a fine sieve into a large bowl. Remove all fat from the broth first by skimming it with a large metal cooking spoon and then by passing bands of kitchen paper over the surface until it is quite clear. Return to a clean pan and reheat to boiling point.

Meanwhile heat a tureen and place the *croûtons* in the bottom, 4 or 5 for each person. Pour the boiling broth over them and serve immediately.

Even the carcass of one roast chicken can make a good *bouillon de poulet*, either for serving before a cold meal or for making sauces and casserole dishes.

Bouillon de poulet
(Chicken Bouillon)
Makes about 600 ml (1 pint)

carcass of 1 roast chicken (skin and debris
   included)
15 g ($\frac{1}{2}$ oz) butter
1 large onion
2 cloves
1 carrot
1.2 litres (2 pints) water
1 teaspoon salt
4 black peppercorns
1 bay leaf
1 sprig parsley
1 small sprig thyme

Break up the carcass into small pieces, melt the butter. Brush the bones lightly with melted butter and place in the bottom of the oven when in use for other cooking. If needed quickly they can be lightly browned under the grill at low heat. Watch carefully that they do not burn. When well-coloured, leave to cool.

Meanwhile, peel the onion, cut into halves and stick a clove into each one. Peel and finely slice the carrot. Put the bones into a large pan, add the water (and a little more if the bones are not covered), add salt and bring slowly to near-boiling point over low heat. Skim off the froth as it rises, and when simmering and the water is clear, add the reserved skin and other debris, onion, carrot and peppercorns, and the herbs tied together. Cover and cook very slowly for 1$\frac{1}{2}$ hours, either over a low heat or in the bottom of the oven.

Remove the lid, increase the heat and continue simmering and reducing for a further 20 minutes. By this time the *bouillon* should have reduced by half.

Strain into a large bowl and leave to cool.

Remove all fat from the surface first with a metal cooking spoon and then by passing bands of kitchen paper over it until clear.

To serve, reheat in a clean pan and pour into small soup-cups. Keep refrigerated for other use.

One of the best country soups is made very simply with chervil. This herb grows like a weed once sown (see page 11) but if chervil is not available the same soup is equally delicious made with either parsley or watercress.

Potage au cerfeuil
(Chervil Soup)
Serves 4

450 g (1 lb) potatoes
1.2 litres (2 pints) water
1 teaspoon salt
4 large handfuls chervil
black pepper
25 g (1 oz) butter
4 tablespoons single cream or top of the milk

Peel the potatoes, wash and cut into quarters and put them into a large pan with the water and salt. Place over medium heat and bring slowly to boiling point. Skim off any froth that rises. When clear, increase the heat slightly and boil rapidly for 10 minutes, uncovered.

Meanwhile wash the chervil under running water, shake off the excess and, after putting the herb into a clean kitchen towel, gather up the corners and swing it round to expel as much moisture as possible. Place in a mug, snip up finely with scissors, stalks as well, and set aside.

Now reduce the heat under the potatoes

and simmer until they start to fall apart. Then increase the heat and boil rapidly for 3 or 4 minutes to reduce the liquid a little. While still boiling, mash the potatoes to a purée with a potato masher. Draw the pan away from the heat, stir in the chopped chervil, add pepper and more salt if necessary, cover and leave until required. This extracts the flavour without discolouring the herb.

To serve, reheat *slowly* until the first bubbles rise, stirring occasionally. Put a small knob of butter and a spoonful of cream into each heated soup-plate, pour in the soup and serve immediately.

When using either parsley or watercress for this recipe, pick off the leaves after washing and shaking, tie the stalks together, cook them with the potatoes, removing them when the potatoes are cooked. Add the chopped leaves as previously indicated.

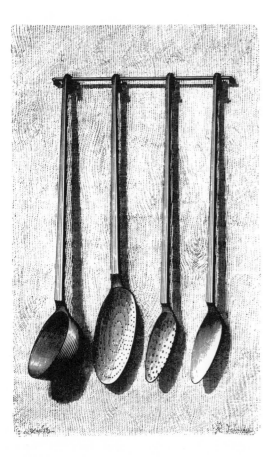

In Lorraine, famous for its beautiful farm-houses and kitchens with huge open fires, its good food and fruit-flavoured *eau-de-vie*, cherries are used for making not only *vin de cerises*, but also soup of a very special and very delicious kind. Wine served hot has added potency and this soup produces a hilarious atmosphere to follow.

Potage aux cerises
(Cherry Soup)
Serves 4

1 kg (2 lb) ripe black cherries
15 g ($\frac{1}{2}$ oz) unsalted butter
2 teaspoons flour
750 ml ($1\frac{1}{4}$ pints) good red wine (claret or burgundy)
sugar
25 ml/1 fl oz kirsch
4 tablespoons fried *croûtons* (see page 33)

Wash and dry the cherries and remove the stalks. Melt the butter in a *sauteuse* or large iron frying pan over medium heat and when foaming add the cherries spread out in one layer. Reduce the heat to low and cook slowly, shaking the pan frequently, until the cherries soften and start to colour lightly. Sprinkle with flour and stir well to distribute it evenly, add the wine and a little sugar. Stir to incorporate the flour, cover and leave to simmer for 30 minutes.

To serve, mix in the kirsch, place the hot *croûtons* in the bottom of each heated bowl and pour the wine and cherries over them. Serve immediately.

The wine used *must* be a good one.

The north-west coastal areas of France produce splendid cockles which are the main ingredient of a well-known fish soup.

Soupe aux coques
(Cockle Soup)
Serves 6

1.2 litres (2 pints) cockles
3 large leeks (white part only)
350 g (12 oz) floury potatoes
40 g (1½ oz) butter
1 litre (1¾ pints) warm water
salt, white pepper
2 medium sized egg yolks
6 tablespoons double cream

Scrub the cockles and wash thoroughly in several changes of cold water. Trim and clean the leeks and slice finely. Peel the potatoes and cut into thin slices.

Melt the butter in a large soup-pan over medium heat and when foaming cook the vegetables slowly without colouring, stirring frequently. Add the warm water and simmer slowly until the potatoes are soft enough to crush. During this time put the cockles into a dry pan over high heat and shake the pan until they open. As they do so, take them out of the pan and remove them from their shells, then set aside, leaving the liquor to settle in the pan. Pour the liquor through a sieve lined with tissues (which will retain any sand) and set aside. Pass the soup and vegetables through a vegetable mill or reduce to purée in an electric blender, season lightly with very little salt and some pepper. Add the cockle liquor and enough hot water to make up the quantity of soup to 2 litres (3½ pints).

When ready to serve, beat the egg yolks and cream together in a small bowl, bring the soup to boiling point, draw the pan from the heat and add the cockles. Stir well, beat a ladleful of soup gradually into the eggs and cream, pour this mixture back into the pan slowly, stir until slightly thickened and serve immediately in well heated soup-cups.

Potage aux haricots
(Haricot Bean Soup)
Serves 6

225 g (8 oz) dried haricot beans
2.5 litres (4 pints) cold water
1 sprig each thyme, parsley, rosemary
1 bay leaf
1 medium sized onion
1 clove garlic
1 small head of celery
2 large leeks
50 g (2 oz) butter
700 g (1½ lb) large tomatoes (preferably Mediterranean variety)
salt, black pepper
2 large eggs

Soak the beans overnight in cold water. Drain and wash them, drain again and place in a large soup-pan with the water. Tie the herbs together with a piece of string, leaving one long end, and add to the pan; tie the long end of string to the pan-handle. Peel onion and garlic and add to pan, but do not add any salt as this would make the beans tough. Bring slowly to boiling point over medium heat. When boiling steadily reduce the heat and simmer for about 1½ hours until the beans are almost tender.

Meanwhile clean and trim the celery and leeks: Cut the dark green leaves off the leeks (which can be used for another soup), and slice the white and pale green parts thickly. Cut the celery into the same sized pieces. Melt half the butter in a wide-based pan and cook these vegetables slowly without colouring, stirring occasionally. When they are tender, add the tomatoes cut into small pieces without skinning. Mix well, season, cover and leave to simmer gently for a further 30 minutes.

Remove the onion and herbs from the soup-pan and add the tomato mixture. Stir well and cook together for 10 minutes. Pass the soup through a *mouli-légumes* or vegetable mill fitted with the medium grid. Correct the seasoning, return the soup to the pan and bring back to boiling point, stirring occasionally. Soften the remaining butter in a warm bowl and beat with a fork until creamy. Add the eggs and beat until incorporated.

To serve, draw the pan away from the heat, gradually stir a ladleful of soup into the egg mixture, mix well and stir this binding back into the pan little by little until thoroughly incorporated. Do not boil again.

Pour immediately into heated soup-plates or bowls and serve without delay.

To reheat any soup left over, pour it into a jug and stand it in a pan half-full of simmering water for 15 minutes.

There are a few dishes which improve with reheating, and the following soup is one of them. The recipe is therefore given in large quantity because it can be frozen without detriment and provides a good stand-by for a quick snack.

Soupe purée de lentilles au riz
(Lentil and Rice Soup)
Serves 6–8

1 large leek
2 cloves garlic
2 large carrots
1 large onion
2 cloves
450 g (1 lb) lentils
3 litres (5 pints) cold water
3 litres (5 pints) hot water
1 tablespoon salt
black pepper
500 ml (18 fl oz) boiling water
225 g (8 oz) rice
25 g (1 oz) butter

Trim the leek, retaining all edible green leaves, and wash well to free from grit. Peel the garlic and carrots and chop them medium-fine together with the leek. Peel the onion, cut into halves and stick a clove into each one.

Put the lentils into a large soup-pan, add the cold water and bring very slowly to boiling point. Boil steadily for 2 or 3 minutes, drain through a sieve, put the lentils back into the pan, add the hot water, salt, pepper and prepared vegetables. Bring to boiling point over medium heat, remove any froth that rises with a slotted spoon, then reduce the heat and simmer steadily, uncovered, for about 1 hour until lentils and vegetables are tender.

Meanwhile butter the rim of another pan to prevent boiling over, pour in the boiling water, add salt and when boiling fast scatter in the rice and cook uncovered for 20 minutes.

Remove the onion halves from the other pan, pick out the cloves and return the onion to the pan. Pass the entire contents through a vegetable mill or reduce to purée in an electric blender. Pour the purée back into the pan, correct the seasoning, and set over very low heat.

Drain the rice, reserving the water. Add the rice to the lentil soup and dilute to the required thickness with the reserved cooking liquid. Correct the seasoning and bring to full boiling point.

To serve, beat in the butter cut into small pieces and when melted ladle the soup into heated soup-plates. Serve very hot with baked garlic-flavoured *croûtons* (see page 33).

Potage au lièvre
(Hare Soup)
Serves 6

bones, head and debris of 1 hare
1 large onion
4 cloves
1 large carrot
2.5 litres (4 pints) water
salt, black pepper
2 bay leaves
2 sprigs parsley
1 sprig thyme
2–3 tablespoons stale brown breadcrumbs
200 ml (6 fl oz) port or 2 lemons

Put the bones, head and debris of the hare into a large soup-pan, add the peeled onion cut into quarters with the cloves stuck into them, the peeled and chopped carrot and the water. Bring slowly to simmering point and skim off the froth as it rises, adding a little cold water each time to make it rise again. When clear, add salt and pepper, and the herbs tied together. Cover and simmer slowly over very low heat for 3 hours. The soup-pan can also be placed in the bottom of the oven during other cooking.

When the meat left on the bones falls away from them and the soup has reduced by half, strain it into a clean pan, pick over the contents of the strainer removing all the bones (especially the very thin rib bones) and either pound the meat to a paste with a wooden spoon or put it in the electric blender with a few tablespoons of liquid. Add this paste to the soup and stir well. Test for seasoning and correct if necessary.

Now add about 1 tablespoon fine breadcrumbs for every 600 ml (1 pint) soup and bring slowly to boiling point again. Simmer for 30 minutes, then whisk the soup vigorously with a hand whisk, or mix in an electric blender and return to the pan to reheat. Remove the pan from the heat and add port. Stir well and serve immediately. Do not let the soup boil again after the port is added.

If no port is available, pour 1 teaspoon lemon juice into each soup-plate before ladling in the soup and serve lemon segments for more juice to be added if required.

French farming families enjoy their soup poured boiling hot over crusts or slices of coarse country bread baked hard. This may seem strange to English taste, until one realises that hard-baked bread is the origin of the more sophisticated fried *croûton*. Bread used for baked *croûtons* should be stale. The kind that most resembles the slightly sour *pain de campagne* eaten in France is light rye bread. Alternatively coarse wholemeal bread may be used.

Potage crème de navets
(Cream of Turnip Soup)
Serves 4

450 g (1 lb) small turnips
25 g (1 oz) butter
1 teaspoon coarse sea salt
225 g (8 oz) floury potatoes
900 ml (1½ pints) water
black pepper, nutmeg
300 ml (½ pint) milk
4 tablespoons single cream
1 tablespoon chopped parsley
12 baked *croûtons* (see page 33)

Peel the turnips and cut them into small chunks. Melt the butter in a soup-pan and when foaming add the turnips and cook slowly over low heat, turning them over until coated with butter. Add salt, cover and cook without colouring for 10 minutes. Meanwhile peel the potatoes and cut into small chunks. Add the water to the turnips and mix well, add potatoes, season with pepper and grated nutmeg, cover and cook slowly for 30 minutes after boiling point is reached. Uncover and allow to reduce for 10 minutes over slightly increased heat.

Pass the contents of the pan through a *mouli-légumes* or reduce to purée in an electric blender, add the milk and reheat to boiling point.

Test for seasoning, correct if necessary and stir in the cream and chopped parsley.

Remove the pan from the heat, stir the soup well and pour over the *croûtons* in well-heated soup-plates. Serve immediately.

The onion soup for which the wholesale food markets of Paris are famous has a brown crusted top known as a *gratinée*. This is made by thickly scattering a large slice of bread with grated gruyère cheese, floating one on each bowl of soup to cover the contents, and toasting it under the grill until crisp and brown. Its country cousin owes the absence of a *gratinée* to the parsimonious nature of the country woman who replaces it by an equally savoury but less costly garnish of finely chopped garlic and parsley. This is known on the farms of Poitou as a *gringot*.

Soupe à l'oignon de Poitou
(Poitou Onion Soup)
Serves 6

3 large cloves garlic
4 tablespoons roughly chopped parsley
12 large Spanish onions
75 g (3 oz) butter
salt, black pepper
2 tablespoons flour
1.5 litres (2½ pints) water
6 thin slices stale rye bread
150 ml (¼ pint) double cream

To make the *gringot*, peel the garlic and chop roughly, add the parsley and chop finely together. Place in a small bowl, cover and set aside.

Peel and chop the onions very finely. Melt the butter in a large pan over medium heat and when foaming add the onions, season and mix well with a wooden spoon. Cook until the onions reach the golden stage, stirring constantly and watching carefully so that they do not burn. Sprinkle with flour and stir to incorporate it into the butter and onions, then add the water. Beat the ingredients well with a hand whisk to prevent lumps forming and bring to boiling point. Boil steadily for 30 minutes and correct the seasoning if necessary. Meanwhile toast the bread lightly on both sides, halve the slices, place in the bottom of a well-heated tureen or large earthenware bowl and keep hot in a moderate oven. Put the cream into a warm bowl.

To serve, draw the pan from the heat, stir a ladleful of soup into the cream and add this gradually to the soup, stirring constantly.

Reheat gently until boiling point is reached and pour over the toasted bread. Cover, and put back in the oven for 5 minutes for the toast to imbibe the flavours.

Serve immediately in very hot soup-plates with the *gringot* sprinkled thickly on top.

This soup is a meal in itself and needs only fresh fruit to follow.

Potage à l'oseille fermière
(Farmhouse Sorrel Soup)
Serves 6

225 g (8 oz) sorrel
1 lettuce
225 g (8 oz) floury potatoes
50 g (2 oz) butter
1.5 litres (2½ pints) water
salt, black pepper, nutmeg
8 chipolata sausages
150 ml (¼ pint) milk
4 tablespoons double cream

Wash and pick over the sorrel but do not remove the centre rib if tender. Drain well. Wash and trim the lettuce retaining all edible outside leaves. Shred finely and set aside. Peel the potatoes and cut into very small chunks.

Melt the butter in a large pan over low heat and when foaming throw in the sorrel and stir rapidly with a wooden spoon until it changes colour. Add the shredded lettuce, stir well and cook until the mixture forms a soft mass. Add water, salt, pepper, grated nutmeg and potatoes, cover and leave to simmer for 30 minutes. Add the chipolatas and cook for a further 10 minutes.

Remove the chipolatas and keep hot. Pass the soup through a vegetable mill or reduce to purée in an electric blender, pour back into the pan. Stir in the milk and heat slowly to boiling point.

To serve, draw the pan from the heat when boiling, mix a little soup into the cream, stir it into the pan, cut the chipolatas into 2 cm (1 inch) pieces, return them to the soup and serve immediately.

Crisply grilled bacon may be substituted for the chipolatas, crumbled over the soup when served (see page 33).

Long slow cooking is, in general, the secret of a good dish. This was always the method used in French kitchens when the flat-topped iron stove reigned supreme. Although it has been generally usurped by modern electric or gas cookers, many farmers' wives have clung to their old solid fuel stoves. Once prepared, the soup-pot simmers on the stove for hours and the meal is ready when they return from the fields. Without this advantage delicious soup can still be made by leaving the pot in the bottom of the oven when it is in use for other cooking, or it can be left overnight in the slow oven of a cooking range and be all the better for being reheated when required.

Soupe à la paysanne
(Mixed Vegetable Soup)
Serves 6–8

1 large onion
1 large leek
2 large carrots
4 small young turnips
3 medium sized potatoes
1 small green cabbage
225 g (8 oz) green beans (French or young runner beans)
175 g (6 oz) pickled belly of pork (see page 83)
1 clove garlic
1 tablespoon pork dripping
about 3 litres (5 pints) warm water
black pepper

Peel and coarsely chop the onion. Trim and clean the leek and slice thinly, all edible green parts included. Peel and dice the carrots and peel and cut the turnips into little chunks. Peel and finely slice the potatoes and leave in a bowl of cold water. Trim and quarter the cabbage, remove the core, and shred finely. Remove strings from the beans if necessary and break into short lengths. Remove the rind from the pork and chop the meat roughly, add the onions and leek and peeled garlic and chop these ingredients together very finely.

Melt the dripping in a large soup-pan and when hot add the chopped pork and onions and cook over low heat for 10 minutes without colouring, stirring frequently. Then add all the other vegetables except the potatoes and beans, cover well with warm water, season with pepper only, and increase the heat to medium. When boiling steadily reduce the heat, cover and simmer very slowly for $2\frac{1}{2}$ to 3 hours. Thirty minutes before serving add the potatoes and beans and correct the seasoning.

When ready to serve crush some of the potatoes and turnips against the side of the pan with a large wooden spoon and pour the soup into heated soup-bowls.

Serve with French bread crisped for 5 minutes in a hot oven.

On farms where eggs and cream are plentiful it is not judged extravagant to include them in the soup. This turns a humble dish into a highly nutritious meal.

Potage crème de poireaux à l'ancienne
(Old-fashioned Cream of Leek Soup)
Serves 6

6 large leeks
50 g (2 oz) butter
salt, black pepper
100 g (4 oz) stale light rye bread
1.2–1.5 litres ($2\frac{1}{4}$ pints) warm water
2 large egg yolks
150 ml ($\frac{1}{4}$ pint) double cream

Trim, clean and wash the leeks thoroughly. Cut off the dark green leaves (which can be used for another soup). Slice the white and pale green parts finely.

Melt the butter in a large soup-pan over medium heat. When foaming add the leeks, season with salt, stir well and cover. Reduce the heat and cook slowly for 15 minutes until they have rendered their juices without colouring. Stir occasionally.

Meanwhile soak the bread in cold water for a few minutes, then squeeze out water. Add the warm water to the leeks, crumble the bread finely into the pan, season well with a little more salt and plenty of pepper, stir well and bring slowly to boiling point. Cover and leave to simmer gently for 45 minutes, stirring occasionally.

Strain the soup into a large bowl, working the solid ingredients through the sieve with a wooden spoon to obtain sufficient purée to thicken it slightly, bearing in mind the egg and cream binding which will thicken the soup further; or reduce one or two ladlesful to purée in a blender. Return this mixture to the pan and bring slowly to boiling point.

Beat the egg yolks and cream together in a small bowl, draw the pan from the heat, stir well, add a ladleful of soup to the bowl a little at a time, stir until incorporated and pour this binding into the soup gradually, stirring meanwhile until thickened. Do not boil again after the yolks are added. Serve immediately in very hot soup-plates.

This soup can be made more economically by replacing the egg yolks and cream with milk and butter. Add 150 ml ($\frac{1}{4}$ pint) milk to the strained soup when it is returned to the pan, simmer until boiling and beat in 25 g (1 oz) butter cut into small pieces. Serve with fried *croûtons* (see page 33).

Soupe aux pois et au lard
(Pea Soup with Bacon)
Serves 6

225 g (8 oz) split peas
450 g (1 lb) leeks
225 g (8 oz) carrots
1 lettuce
225 g (8 oz) lean streaky bacon (in one piece)
2 teaspoons salt
3 litres (5 pints) cold water
black pepper
1 sprig each parsley, thyme, rosemary
1 bay leaf
450 g (1 lb) floury potatoes
6 thin slices stale rye or wholemeal bread
6 tablespoons double cream (optional)

Soak the peas in cold water overnight. Drain and wash in cold water before cooking.

Trim, clean and cut the leeks into thick slanting slices, all edible green parts included. Peel the carrots and slice thinly. Trim and wash the lettuce. Cut the bacon into thick finger-sized pieces and put these into a large soup-pan. Add the peas, leeks, carrots and salt, cover with water and place over medium heat. Bring slowly to boiling point and skim off the froth as it rises. When the surface is clear, add pepper, and the herbs tied together. Cover, reduce the heat and simmer slowly for 1½ hours until the peas are almost cooked. Meanwhile peel the potatoes and cut them into small chunks. Shred the lettuce finely and add it with the potatoes to the pan. Simmer for a further 30 minutes, uncovered.

Test for seasoning and correct if necessary. Remove the herbs. Cut the slices of bread across twice diagonally, if they are large, place in the bottom of a heated tureen or large earthenware bowl and pour the soup over them. Cover and place in a moderate oven for 5 minutes to soak the bread. Serve in well-heated soup-plates. A spoonful of cream may be stirred into each plateful if desired.

Potage aux topinambours
(Jerusalem Artichoke Soup)
Serves 6

2 large onions
2 medium sized floury potatoes
1 medium sized leek
1 branch celery
1 sprig parsley
2 cloves
450 g (1 lb) Jerusalem artichokes
50 g (2 oz) butter
2.5 litres (4 pints) water
coarse sea salt, black pepper
3 small egg yolks
3 tablespoons cream
1 teaspoon soft butter

Peel and slice the onions. Peel the potatoes and wrap them in a wet cloth until required. Trim and wash the leek, celery and parsley, tie them into a bundle and stick the cloves into the leek. Peel and finely slice the artichokes. Melt the butter in a large soup-pan over medium heat. Add the onions, stir well to coat with butter and cook slowly until slightly softened without colouring them. Add the artichokes and cook until soft, stirring occasionally. Pour the water over them, add the potatoes cut into small chunks, season well and put the bundle of flavouring vegetables into the pan. Bring to boiling point, boil steadily for 2 or 3 minutes, reduce the heat and simmer slowly for 45 minutes, uncovered.

When the vegetables are soft and the liquid reduced, remove the bundle of vegetables and discard them. Pass the soup through a *mouli-légumes* or reduce to purée in an electric blender, and reheat to boiling point. Test for seasoning and correct if necessary.

Beat the egg yolks, cream and soft butter together in a small bowl, draw the pan from the heat, add a ladleful of soup slowly to the mixture, stirring constantly, then pour it gradually into the soup and mix well. Do not allow to boil again after this binding is added. Serve with fried *croûtons* (see page 33).

Hot red wine is regarded by Frenchmen as the best means of keeping out the cold. Farmers start the day warm and snug by taking this inspired concoction for breakfast. For less robust constitutions it makes an excellent nightcap.

La trempine
(Hot Wine Soup)
Serves 6

1 large piece rye or wholemeal breadcrust
12 large sugar lumps
200 ml (6 fl oz) boiling water
1 litre (1¾ pints) strong red wine
1 stick cinnamon or 2 teaspoons ground
    cinnamon
2 teaspoons sugar

Cut the breadcrust into 12 short lengths the size of the thumb and bake until dry under a low grill.

Heat the oven to 140°C, 275°F, Gas 1 with 6 small earthenware bowls inside.

When the oven is warm place two pieces of breadcrust in each bowl, put two lumps of sugar on top and pour the boiling water over them. Put back in the oven to keep hot.

Pour the wine into an enamel-lined saucepan, add the cinnamon and sugar and place over a low heat. When warm, test for flavouring, adding more cinnamon or sugar according to taste, allowing for the sugar in the bowls.

Heat slowly until very hot when tested with a knuckle joint. The wine must not boil.

Pour steaming over the *croûtons* in the hot bowls and serve immediately, but not too liberally to the uninitiated.

A *potée*, one of France's great country dishes, is a hearty soup that makes a meal in itself. *Potées* consist of pork, vegetables and savoury herbs which simmer very slowly to produce meltingly tender meat and a delicious broth. This very satisfying winter dish varies according to region. Sometimes the meat, vegetables and broth are served all together in large soupplates, sometimes the broth is served separately, or the broth can be reserved to serve another day with a less hearty meal.

In Bourgogne the farmer's wife continues making her *potée* until the spring when young vegetables fresh from the garden give a new interest to the various kinds of pickled pork that are the mainstay of her larder.

Potée bourguignonne
(Potée with Pickled Pork)
Serves 8–10

½ pickled pig's head
450 g (1 lb) lean pickled belly of pork (see
    page 83)
2 pig's trotters (split lengthways)
225 g (8 oz) lean green boiling bacon (in one
    piece)
2 medium sized onions
2 cloves
1 bay leaf
1 large sprig thyme
8 black peppercorns
6 white peppercorns
225 g (8 oz) each young carrots, very small
    turnips, green haricot beans, green peas
    (shelled)
450 g (1 lb) firm hearted cabbage
salt
450 g (1 lb) small new potatoes

recipe continues overleaf

Wash the pig's head and belly of pork well under cold running water. Put into a very large soup-pan, cover generously with cold water, bring *slowly* to boiling point over low heat and boil steadily for 5 minutes. Drain the meats thoroughly, wash in warm water, clean out the soup-pan and put the meats back into it. Add the trotters and boiling bacon and cover with cold water. Bring slowly to boiling point and skim off the froth as it rises. Meanwhile peel the onions and stick the cloves into them. Tie the bay leaf and thyme together. When the surface of the liquid is clear add the onions and herbs to the pan. Add the peppercorns but do not add salt until later. Cover the pan and leave to simmer gently for 2 hours.

Meanwhile wash and peel the carrots and turnips. Cut the carrots into serving pieces, quarter the turnips, wash and trim the beans and cabbage. Cut the beans into short lengths and cut the cabbage into 8 sections. Add all these vegetables to the pan, with a little salt if the *bouillon* requires it. If the ingredients are not covered add just enough boiling water to cover and simmer without a lid for 45 minutes after boiling point returns. Scrape the potatoes, add to the pan after this time has elapsed and boil for a further 15 minutes. Add the peas and cook for another 15 minutes or until they are tender.

To serve, remove the pig's head and trotters with a slotted spoon, leaving the *potée* gently simmering without a lid. Remove all bones, skin the tongue, cut the meat into pieces and place in a deep dish over a panful of boiling water. Cover with foil to keep hot. Remove the rest of the meat from the pan, cut into thick slices and keep hot.

Ladle the vegetables and *bouillon* into deep, well-heated soup-plates, arrange a little of each of the meats on top and serve very hot with strong French mustard handed separately.

Traditionally a good red burgundy accompanies this dish so that a little wine poured into the half-emptied plate helps to make room for the second helping, or so Burgundians say.

Potée fraîche
(Potée with Fresh Pork)
Serves 6

1.5 kg (3 lb) fresh blade of pork
6 carrots
6 small turnips
4 medium sized onions
1 clove garlic
4 cloves
1 head of celery
8 black peppercorns
1 knuckle of ham (unsalted)
1 bay leaf
1 sprig each thyme, rosemary
1½ teaspoons salt
1 kg (2¼ lb) firm hearted cabbage
10 medium sized potatoes
1 tablespoon chopped parsley
12–18 small baked *croûtons* (see page 33)
2 tablespoons cream (optional)
lemon juice (optional)

Ask the butcher to bone the pork and tie the meat into a neat shape.

Wash and peel the carrots, turnips, onions and garlic and leave them whole. Stick a clove into each onion. Trim the celery, remove damaged outside leaves and cut through the heart into quarters. Cut into three down the length and tie into bundles. Crush the peppercorns.

Put the meats into a very large soup-pan and cover generously with cold water. Place over moderate heat and bring slowly to boiling point. Skim off any froth that rises to the surface and when it is quite clear add the prepared vegetables, herbs tied together, peppercorns and salt. Alternatively, omit the herbs, peppercorns and salt and instead add 2 teaspoons spiced salt (see page 15). When boiling point is reached reduce the heat to low, cover and simmer very gently for 1¼ hours.

Meanwhile, trim the cabbage, cut into 8 sections, remove the inner core leaving just enough to hold the leaves together and place in a large pan. Cover with boiling water, boil for 5 minutes, drain well and add to the other vegetables after they have cooked for 1 hour. Add a little boiling water if they are not covered. Test for seasoning, correct if necessary and cook for a further hour or until the meats are tender.

During this time peel the potatoes and cook them in a separate pan so that they are ready to serve when the *potée* is cooked.

To serve, drain the meat and vegetables well, reserving the broth. Discard the bundle of herbs if used. Remove the cloves from the onions. Carve the meat into thick slices and arrange on a heated serving dish with the vegetables in groups around. Sprinkle with chopped parsley, cover with foil and keep hot in a warm oven.

Pour the soup into a wide-topped bowl and remove the fat first with a large metal cooking spoon, then by passing bands of kitchen paper over the surface until clear. Reheat to boiling point in a clean pan, and pour into heated soup-cups over 2 or 3 *croûtons*. A teaspoonful of cream into which a few drops of lemon juice have been stirred may be added to each serving if desired.

Serve the soup at the same time as the meat and vegetables. Strong French mustard and small pickled gherkins are handed separately.

Garnishes

Crisp bacon
Crisply grilled streaky bacon rashers, crumbled and sprinkled, hot, over vegetable soup. Allow one rasher for each person.

Baked croûtons
Those used in country soups are usually short thick lengths of breadcrust baked in the oven until hard and crisp. The hot soup is poured over them. Allow two or three for each person. They can also be flavoured with garlic by rubbing the cut clove over them before baking. These *croûtons* can be made when the oven is in use for other cooking. When cool, they can be stored in an airtight tin.

Fried croûtons
Cut stale white bread into slices 1 cm ($\frac{1}{2}$ inch) thick, remove the crusts, cut into 1 cm ($\frac{1}{2}$ inch) strips and then into cubes. Sauté in foaming butter until crisp and golden on all sides, shaking the pan frequently. Drain on kitchen paper and serve hot. Allow half a slice of bread for each person. These *croûtons* can be made in advance, stored in an airtight box and reheated in the oven when required. Do not store for more than a week.

Chervil
Finely chopped chervil sprinkled over vegetable soup just before serving and stirred in gives an appetising flavour. Allow 2 teaspoons chopped chervil for each helping.

Gruyère cheese and parsley
Equal quantities of grated gruyère cheese and finely chopped parsley mixed together and handed separately, for sprinkling over the soup when served. Allow 2 teaspoons for each helping.

Hard-boiled egg and parsley
Two tablespoons finely chopped parsley to each finely chopped hard-boiled egg, mixed together, seasoned with salt and pepper and handed separately, for sprinkling over the soup when served. Allow 2 teaspoons for each helping.

Mint
Although mint is rarely used in French cooking it makes a delicious garnish for a mixed vegetable soup. Allow 1 teaspoon finely chopped mint for each large helping.

Chapter Three

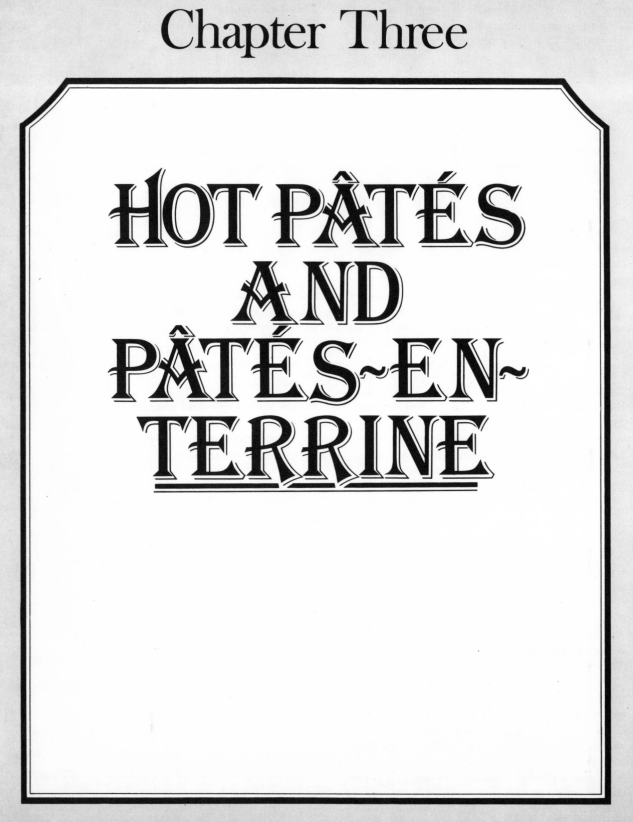

HOT PÂTÉS AND PÂTÉS-EN-TERRINE

The ingenuity displayed by French country people when it comes to not wasting anything edible is impressive.

On the farms of Vendée, when a pig is slaughtered and the black puddings are made, even the water in which they were boiled is shared with appreciative neighbours. Spangled with scraps of filling escaped from the skins, it is made into a soup called *soupe à la boudine* which they relish greatly.

This same ingenuity is allowed free reign when it comes to making *pâtés*.

Hot Pâtés

Pâtés of a special kind served hot are a feature of country menus. This one is served as a main course:

Pâté de ma grand-mère
(Hot Liver Pâté)
Serves 4–5

100 g (4 oz) chicken livers
350 g (12 oz) pig's liver
1 clove garlic or 3 shallots
2 tablespoons chopped parsley
3 medium sized eggs
25 g (1 oz) butter
25 g (1 oz) flour
600 ml (1 pint) milk
1½ teaspoons salt
½ teaspoon each black pepper, nutmeg
¼ teaspoon white pepper
a 1 litre (2 pint) *soufflé* dish

Remove all membrane and parts stained yellow on the chicken livers—they give a bitter flavour to the dish. Remove any membrane from the pig's liver by sliding the sharp point of a knife under it and slicing along underneath. Peel the garlic or shallots and chop roughly. Cut the livers into small pieces and mix with the garlic or shallots and the parsley.

Put the mixture twice through the mincer, or blend in the electric blender. Beat the eggs in a mixing bowl and add the blended livers. Melt the butter in a large saucepan, stir in the flour and mix well over a gentle heat for a minute before adding the milk. Beat with a hand whisk until smooth and cook, stirring constantly, until thick and bubbling. Continue simmering and stirring for 3 minutes. Remove the pan from the heat, beat in the liver mixture and season well.

Butter the *soufflé* dish thickly and pour in the *pâté* mixture, cover with a piece of well-buttered greaseproof paper, then a piece of cooking foil and tie them round the dish. Pierce the centre with a pointed knife and make a small hole. Cut a strip of foil 5 cm (2 inches) wide, wind it round a pencil to make a small funnel and insert it in the hole. Stand this dish in a baking tin half full of hot water, and cook in the oven at 190°C, 375°F, Gas 5, for 1¼ hours, replenishing the hot water in the tin if it evaporates.

The *pâté* is cooked when a metal skewer or knitting needle plunged down the funnel comes out clean. If not, cook for a further 15 minutes.

To unmould, leave to settle for a few minutes, then pass a thin-bladed knife round the inside of the dish, place a heated serving plate on top, and quickly invert the *pâté* on to it.

Serve at once with *coulis de tomates* handed separately (see overleaf).

What is left over can be pressed into a smaller dish just large enough to hold it and when cold covered with foil and refrigerated. Serve cut into slices with a green salad.

Previous page: *Pâté-terrine de poisson* (see page 43).
Opposite: *Croustade florentine* (see page 48).

Coulis de tomates
(Fresh Tomato Sauce)

700 g (1½ lb) large ripe tomatoes
225 g (8 oz) onions
1 clove garlic
2 tablespoons olive oil
salt, black pepper, sugar
1 tablespoon chopped basil

Prick the tomatoes in several places, plunge them into boiling water for 1 minute and then into cold. Skin and chop roughly. Peel the onions and chop finely. Peel and crush the garlic.

Put the olive oil into a large pan over medium heat, add the onions and mix well. Sprinkle with salt and cook until they become transparent. Add the tomatoes, garlic, more salt, pepper and a large pinch of sugar and cook uncovered until the juice runs from the tomatoes. Continue cooking, stirring occasionally to prevent sticking, and allow to bubble until the liquid is re-absorbed and the mixture reduced to a thick purée. Stir in the basil and pour into a heated sauceboat. If basil is not available tie together 1 sprig each of thyme and rosemary, 1 bay leaf and 1 stalk of celery and cook with the tomatoes. Remove before serving. This purée can be bottled or frozen.

Where hens lay their eggs under every hedgerow a hot *pâté* that calls for eight eggs is not considered extravagant. It is, however, considered a dish for special occasions and is usually served when fish is the main course.

Gâteau de foies de volaille
(Hot Chicken Liver Pâté)
Serves 6

350 g (12 oz) chicken livers
40 g (1½ oz) flour, sieved
4 medium sized eggs
4 medium sized egg yolks
4 tablespoons cream
750 ml (1¼ pints) full-cream milk
salt, pepper, nutmeg
1 teaspoon chopped parsley
½ clove garlic
a 1.5 litre (3 pint) mould or *soufflé* dish

If using frozen chicken livers allow them to thaw at room temperature. Remove any membrane and parts stained yellow, and cut into pieces. Put them, with the thawed-out juices, into an electric blender, add the flour and blend until smooth. Empty this preparation into a mixing bowl and add the whole eggs one at a time, working them in with a wooden spatula. Then add the extra yolks, one at a time. Beat well with a hand whisk adding first the cream, then the milk, salt, pepper, grated nutmeg, chopped parsley, and the peeled and crushed garlic. Work this mixture thoroughly to a smooth cream. To test for seasoning, drop a teaspoonful into a small pan of boiling water and when it rises to the top and is firm, taste and correct if necessary. Heat the oven to 180°C, 350°F, Gas 4.

Butter the mould or *soufflé* dish and pour in the mixture. Place in a baking tin half full of hot water and bring the water to boiling point on top of the cooker. Place immediately in the oven. Cook gently for 45 minutes to 1 hour. When the *gâteau* is cooked it will shrink a little from the sides of the dish and a metal skewer or knitting needle plunged into the centre will come out clean.

To serve, pass a knife blade round the inner rim of the mould, hold a heated serving plate over it, grasp both of them firmly and invert quickly, setting the dish down with a sharp tap to unmould. Serve immediately with the following sauce. Pour a little of the sauce over the *gâteau* and serve the rest in a heated sauceboat. If necessary, the *gâteau* can be kept hot for 10 minutes in the *bain-marie* in the oven with the heat turned off.

Sauce aux champignons
(Mushroom Sauce)

45 g (1¾ oz) butter
20 g (¾ oz) flour
salt, black pepper
400 ml (¾ pint) milk
1 medium sized onion
175 g (6 oz) mushrooms
1–2 teaspoons lemon juice

Melt 20 g (¾ oz) butter in a saucepan over medium heat, work in the flour with a wooden spoon, add salt and pepper and cook until frothy without colouring. Draw the pan away from the heat, add the milk all at once and beat with a wire whisk until smooth. Replace over medium heat and stirring constantly bring to boiling point, reduce the heat and simmer for 5 minutes. Remove from the heat, press a buttered paper on to the surface to prevent a skin forming and set the *béchamel* aside.

Peel and chop the onion; peel and slice the mushrooms. Melt 15 g (½ oz) butter in a small pan and over low heat cook the onion without browning until transparent and tender. Stir occasionally and season lightly. When cooked, remove from the pan and keep warm. In the same pan melt the rest of the butter, add the mushrooms, sprinkle with salt to extract the juice, cover and cook over very low heat until soft. By this time there should be a fair quantity of mushroom essence in the pan. Add this, the mushrooms and the onions to the *béchamel*. Sharpen the flavour with lemon juice to taste. Mix well, test for seasoning, add more pepper if necessary, and cook slowly over gentle heat for 5 minutes, stirring frequently.

Pâtés-en-terrine

It should be noted that the classic *pâtés* served as a first course are, in culinary terms, divided into two categories: *pâtés-en-terrine*, a smooth mixture of minced meats or minced and sliced meats, which are baked in a *terrine* or earthenware dish from which they take their name, and *pâtés-en-croûte*, a coarser mixture of minced and sliced meats baked in a crust. Pork mixtures are mainly baked *en terrine*.

Pâté-terrine de campagne
(Country Pâté, coarse texture)
Serves 14–16

225 g (8 oz) chicken livers
175 g (6 oz) pig's liver
2 shallots
700 g (1½ lb) lean pork (leg or shoulder)
175 g (6 oz) pork fat or fat belly of pork
1½ teaspoons salt
½ teaspoon each black pepper, nutmeg
¼ teaspoon white pepper
2 tablespoons brandy or dry vermouth
40 g (1½ oz) pistachio nuts
225 g (8 oz) streaky bacon rashers
thick flour and water paste for sealing
    (optional)

Trim the chicken livers, removing all parts stained yellow. These give a bitter taste if not removed. Trim the pig's liver of any membrane by inserting the point of a sharp knife under the strip of skin and sliding the knife along to sever it. Peel and roughly chop the shallots and cut pork, fat and livers into small pieces. Put these ingredients through the mincer, add the seasoning and brandy or vermouth and mix thoroughly. Test for seasoning and add more if necessary. Pour boiling water over the nuts, leave for a few minutes then drain and plunge into cold water. Rub off the red skin and cut them into halves. Mix into the *pâté*. Heat the oven to 180°C, 350°F, Gas 4.

If you have no *terrine* or earthenware dish in which a *pâté* is traditionally cooked and served, use an ordinary *soufflé* dish. Line your dish with the rashers of streaky bacon, leaving enough hanging over the side to fold over, and fill with the prepared mixture. Fold the bacon over the surface. If using a *soufflé* dish, cover with a piece of well-buttered greaseproof paper, then a piece of cooking foil and tie them round the dish. Pierce the centre with a pointed knife and make a small hole. Cut a strip of foil 5 cm (2 inches) wide, wind it round a pencil to make a small funnel and insert it in the hole. If you have a *terrine* you are spared this trouble; just cover the prepared meat with the lid and seal it down with flour and water paste shaped into a long roll, having first dampened the edges of the dish with water to make the seal stick.

Put the dish into a baking tin half filled with hot water and place in the bottom half of the oven. Cook for 20 minutes, then reduce the heat to 140°C, 275°F, Gas 1 and continue cooking for 2½ hours. To test, push a metal skewer or knitting needle down the funnel of paper or through the airhole of the lid, and if it comes out clean the *pâté* is done. Remove the lid or cooking foil but not the buttered paper; if using a *terrine*, cover with greaseproof paper. Put a plate or piece of wood on the surface and put a small weight on top of that. Leave to cool completely. This *pâté* keeps very well in the refrigerator and can also be frozen.

Pâté de foie campagnard
(Country Pâté, smooth texture)
Serves 12–14

350 g (12 oz) lean belly of pork (without rind)
450 g (1 lb) pig's liver
100 g (4 oz) gammon rasher (in one piece)
1 tablespoon pure lard or pork dripping
salt, black pepper, nutmeg
2 teaspoons flour
300 ml ($\frac{1}{2}$ pint) hot milk
5 small eggs
225 g (8 oz) fat green streaky bacon (thinly sliced)
a long earthenware 1 litre (2 pint) *pâté* dish

Cut the belly of pork and liver into 2.5 cm (1 inch) cubes. Remove the rind and fat from the gammon and cut the lean into small dice.

In a *sauteuse* or large frying pan, melt the lard or pork dripping over medium heat and when hot add the large pork cubes and sauté until golden. Reduce the heat to low and cook slowly for 20 minutes, turning them occasionally until golden brown on all sides. Remove with a slotted spoon and set aside. Sauté the liver quickly in the same fat for 1 minute only, shaking the pan constantly so that the cubes are just sealed, no more. Mix with the cooked pork. Season well with salt, and pepper and grated nutmeg *or* 1 teaspoon spiced salt (see page 15). Leave to cool.

Make a *panade* or binding by straining the cooking fat into a saucepan, work in the flour and when frothy pour in the hot milk and whisk thoroughly until smooth. Season with salt and pepper. Bring slowly to boiling point, allow to bubble for 1 minute, cover with a buttered paper pressed on to the surface, to prevent a skin forming, and set aside.

Put the cooked meats through the fine grid of the mincer, beat this purée into the *panade* until smooth and add the eggs one at a time, beating constantly. Test for seasoning, adding more pepper and nutmeg or spiced salt. Mix in the diced gammon. Heat the oven to 180°C, 350°F, Gas 4.

Reserving one rasher, line the *pâté* dish with strips of fat streaky bacon leaving the ends overhanging. Pour in the *pâté* mixture, fold over the ends towards each other and cover the centre with the remaining rasher. Place the dish in the oven in a baking tin half full of hot water and cook for 30 minutes. Reduce the heat to 150 °C, 300 °F, Gas 2, and cook for a further 1$\frac{1}{4}$ hours. Remove from the oven and allow to cool for 10 minutes, then press down the surface firmly with the palm of your hand.

Leave for 24 hours in a cool airy place before serving.

To serve, cut the required number of slices and arrange on a serving dish surrounded by lettuce leaves. Cover the cut side of the *pâté* with a sheet of greaseproof paper and refrigerate.

If the *pâté* is to serve 12 or more people at one meal, unmould by running a thin-bladed knife around the inside of the dish, place the serving plate on top and invert the *pâté* on to it. Garnish with sprigs of watercress and black olives.

During the shooting season all that goes into the bag ends up in the *terrine*. The following recipe can be used with rabbits, pheasant or any other game birds instead of hare.

Terrine de lièvre
(Hare Pâté)
Serves 14–16

1 large well-hung hare (about 2–2.5 kg
 [4–5 lb])
325 g (11 oz) shoulder of veal
6 tablespoons brandy
3 tablespoons water
350 g (12 oz) blade of pork (boned)
225 g (8 oz) pork fat or fat belly of pork
1 teaspoon each salt, allspice
½ teaspoon each cinnamon, white pepper
3 bay leaves
2 sprigs thyme
black pepper
6 thin slices of larding fat or 6 rashers fat
 green streaky bacon
thick flour and water paste for sealing

Have the hare paunched, skinned and dressed and the legs and rib cage removed from the saddle. Reserve the heart and liver. Wipe thoroughly with a cloth wrung out in cold water.

Cut the meat from the saddle of the hare in long thin slices parallel to the back bone and cut the veal into the same thin slices. Place them in one layer in a shallow earthenware dish and add the heart and liver. Mix the brandy with the water, pour over the meat, cover and leave to marinate for at least 24 hours. Turn the meat over three times during this period.

Using a small sharp knife cut all the meat from the bones of the hare. Scrape the bones clean and reserve them for soup (see page 26). Remove the rind from the pork. Cut the unmarinated meats, the fat, heart and liver into pieces. Mix them all together and pass them through the fine grid of the mincer.

Season with salt, allspice, cinnamon and white pepper.

Drain the marinated meats but do not dry. Reserve the liquid. Place 2 bay leaves and 1 sprig of thyme cut into pieces in the bottom of a *terrine*, or earthenware *pâté* dish. Cover with a layer of minced meat, then with a layer of hare and veal slices and season these pieces lightly with salt and black pepper. Cover with a layer of minced meat and so on until the dish is full. Press down firmly with the palm of your hand and put the remaining herbs on top. Cover with slices of larding fat or fat bacon and pierce the whole contents of the *terrine* with a sharp skewer in about 12 places. Measure the reserved marinade; there should be about 6 tablespoons; if not, make up the quantity with brandy and a little water. Pour the marinade into the holes.

Shape the flour and water paste into a long roll, wet the rim of the *terrine* and stick the paste on to it. Force the lid of the *terrine* down on to the paste to seal and place in the oven standing in a baking tin half full of hot water. Cook for 30 minutes at 180°C, 350°F, Gas 4, then reduce the heat to 150°C, 300°F, Gas 2, and cook for 3 hours. Remove from oven and leave to cool in the dish for 20 minutes. Remove the lid and paste, and press the *pâté* down firmly with the palm of your hand. When cold, cover with greaseproof paper and leave in a cool place to mature for at least 48 hours before serving.

Serve in the dish, cut across into slices.

If a *terrine* with lid is not available, cook in a *soufflé* dish as advised on page 40.

This *pâté* keeps well when refrigerated or stored in a cool airy larder.

Provençal country people, being in the majority fruit and vegetable farmers, have their own kinds of *pâté* made of olives, which are one of their important products. The traditional *tapenade* includes anchovies, but the lesser known version simply called *pâté d'olives* depends solely on the quality of the fruit for its savour. It is essential for authentic flavour to buy the really black, rather small olives preserved in olive oil and not the large purple-black olives soaked in a vinegar solution which many of our delicatessen shops now seem to favour.

Pâté d'olives
(Black Olive Pâté)
Serves 4

50 g (2 oz) butter
225 g (8 oz) black olives
¼ teaspoon dried powdered thyme or rosemary, or 3 crushed juniper berries
1 small onion
1 small clove garlic

Put the butter in a warm place to soften. Crush the olives lightly with the end of a bottle to free the stones from the flesh. With a sharp pointed knife remove the stones and chop the flesh finely. Add powdered thyme or rosemary, or crushed juniper.

Peel and chop the onion and garlic and pound to a paste in a mortar with the olive flesh. Alternatively they can be passed through the fine grid of a mincing machine. If the latter method is used the mixture must be minced twice to obtain a smooth paste. Now work in the softened butter a little at a time until all is thoroughly blended to a smooth cream. Test for seasoning and add more herbs if necessary. Pack the *pâté* into an earthenware bowl, cover and chill until required.

Serve with thin slices of light rye or brown bread, accompanied by a bottle of chilled Muscadet.

This fish *pâté-en-terrine* has a very subtle and delicious flavour which is at its best the day after it is made. It is not for long keeping and should therefore be consumed within the four or five days following. The bread used in this recipe must be oven-baked (see note on page 8).

Pâté-terrine de poisson
(Fish Pâté)
Serves 12

1 large, thin-skinned lemon
350 g (12 oz) mixed fillets of brill or whiting and fresh haddock
450 g (1 lb) rock-salmon (huss)
salt, black pepper, celery salt
175 g (6 oz) butter
100 g (4 oz) stale white breadcrumbs
3 tablespoons chopped parsley
1 large egg
3 tablespoons milk
lemon slices (optional)
a 1 litre (2 pint) *soufflé* dish

Peel the lemon thinly with a potato peeler and chop the peel very finely. Squeeze and strain the juice. There should be about 4 tablespoonsful.

Ease up the skin from the pointed end of the fish fillets with the thumb-nail and place them on the cutting board pointed end away from you. Holding the skin with a cloth or dipping the fingers in salt will give a good grip. Pull the skin towards you, pressing down on the fish with the blunt edge of a knife. Cut the fish across into thin strips and across again into tiny cubes. Chop finely and set aside.

Lay the rock-salmon on the cutting board and with a sharp knife cut down the length of the backbone pressing the knife close to the bone on each side, separating the fish into long fillets. Cut these across into 1.5 cm (½ inch) wide strips and arrange them in one layer on a large dinner plate. Season with very little salt, plenty of pepper, sprinkle with 2 tablespoons lemon juice and scatter liberally

recipe continues overleaf

with celery salt. Mix well together, spread out, cover and set aside.

Cut the butter into pieces, put it into a mixing bowl and set in a warm place. When soft, beat to a cream with a fork, add 1 teaspoon salt, some pepper and the chopped lemon peel, and beat well. Add the bread-crumbs little by little, beating them in, then add the finely chopped fish, 2 tablespoons chopped parsley and the rest of the lemon juice. Pound this mixture thoroughly with a pestle or a wooden spoon to shred the fish and blend it into the other ingredients. Beat the egg with a pinch of salt and the milk and work it into the *farce* to bind it.

Butter the *soufflé* dish and divide the fillets into two parts and the *farce* into three. Fill the dish first with a layer of *farce*, then a layer of fillets and so on, ending with the *farce*. Press down firmly on the contents of the dish when filled, to prevent cracks forming when cooked. Cover with a sheet of buttered greaseproof paper and then a sheet of foil, both pleated in the centre to allow for expansion. Tie them round the dish. Pierce the centre with a pointed knife and make a small hole. Cut a strip of foil 5 cm (2 inches) wide, wind it round a pencil to make a small funnel and insert it in the hole. Stand the dish in a *bain-marie* or baking tin half full of hot water and cook in the lower half of the oven at 180°C, 350°F, Gas 4 for 1½ hours. When the *pâté* is cooked, half open the oven door and leave the dish inside until it is quite cold. Do not remove the covering until ready to serve.

To serve, remove the foil and paper, wipe around the rim of the dish with a damp cloth, run a knife blade round the *pâté*, turn it out on to a cutting board and cut half of it into 5 mm (¼ inch) thick slices. Cut into halves, arrange on a serving plate and garnish with the re-maining parsley and lemon slices if liked. Return the remainder to the dish, cover and chill for further use.

After serving *pâté-terrine de poisson* cold as a first course, the remainder makes a very delectable main course to serve hot the following day.

Pâté-terrine de poisson chaud
(Fish Pâté, served hot)

half the cold fish *pâté* (see preceding recipe)
100 g (4 oz) gruyère cheese
600 ml (1 pint) *béchamel* sauce (see page 131)
nutmeg, salt, black pepper
2 tablespoons *chapelure* (see page 67)

Cut the *pâté* into slices about 1 cm (½ inch) thick, divide these into halves to make rect-angles and arrange in a buttered fireproof dish in one layer. Grate the cheese and set it aside. Make the *béchamel* sauce as advised, then remove the pan from the heat and add three-quarters of the grated cheese. Beat until the cheese has melted. Add a generous pinch of grated nutmeg, test for seasoning, correct if necessary and pour the sauce over the *pâté* to cover completely. Mix the rest of the cheese with the *chapelure* and scatter it over the sur-face. Place under a pre-heated medium grill to heat the *pâté* through, then increase the heat and grill until the cheese forms a brown crust and the sauce bubbles. Serve immediately.

Christmas is just another working day on a French farm but the New Year is celebrated throughout the country by a splendid dinner on New Year's Eve. It starts early and goes on until New Year's Day has been celebrated, courses following each other endlessly. Townspeople dine out but country cooks start weeks ahead to prepare for the feast that is given at home.

Poultry and game livers are collected well in advance and frozen for making the special *pâté* served at this *réveillon*.

Pâté du réveillon
(Mixed Poultry and Game Liver Pâté)
Serves 18–20

700 g (1½ lb) mixed livers (chicken, duck, turkey, goose and game)
350 g (12 oz) butter
salt, black pepper
1 teaspoon dried savory or marjoram
4 tablespoons brandy

Remove the livers from the deep freeze and place in the refrigerator overnight. Thaw at room temperature 2 or 3 hours before required and reserve the liquid thawed out.

Place the butter in a warm place to soften slightly. Remove all membrane from the livers, and slice off any parts stained yellow as these would give a bitter flavour.

Melt a third of the butter in a large frying pan over a low heat and when foaming add the livers and cook slowly for about 4 minutes, turning them over as they are sealed. Do not overcook. They must remain soft and slightly pink inside. Season well, add the savory or marjoram and mix thoroughly. Pour the brandy into the pan, remove it from the heat, ignite and tilt the pan to keep the flames going, basting the livers at the same time.

Add the liquid reserved after thawing, mix well and pour the contents of the pan into an electric blender. Blend until smooth.

Divide the rest of the butter into small pieces and put them into a warmed earthenware serving bowl. Pour the liver purée over them and beat the mixture thoroughly with a hand whisk to incorporate the butter. Test for seasoning and correct if necessary.

Smooth down the *pâté* with the back of a fork and make a criss-cross pattern on top with the prongs. When cold, refrigerate until required. Leave at room temperature for 30 minutes before serving with thin dry toast. No butter is required.

This is not a long-keeping *pâté* once it has been served. Store in the refrigerator but not longer than 8 to 10 days.

Chapter Four

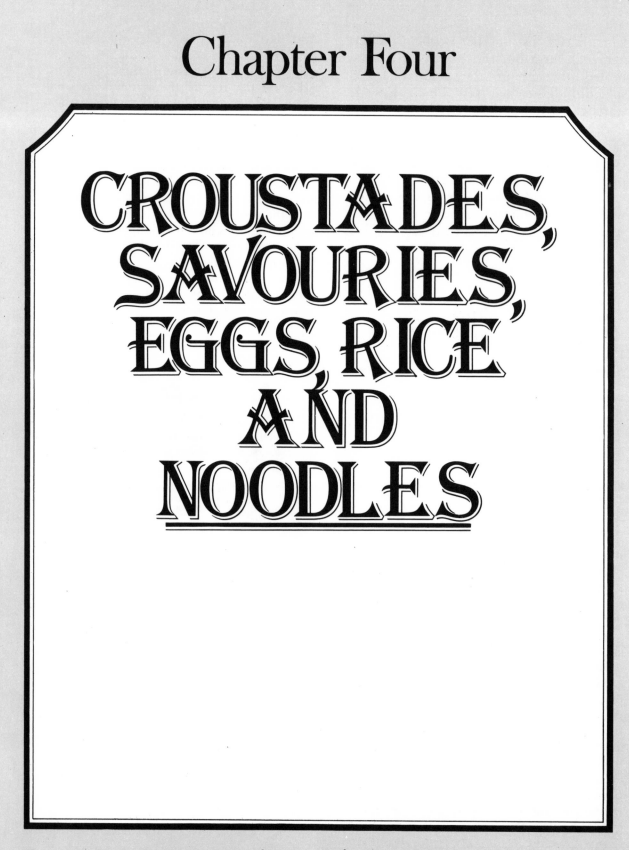

CROUSTADES, SAVOURIES, EGGS RICE AND NOODLES

Croustades

Hot savoury tarts known as *croustades* are a first course speciality of farmhouse Sunday lunches in France. They vary with the region, the family recipe book and the season.

The following *croustade* recipes will serve 4 people as a main course lunch or supper dish when served with a green salad, or 6 people as a first course. For larger numbers use the pastry quantities given for 6–8 and increase the fillings by half.

Pâte brisée
(Shortcrust Pastry)

Serves 4–6

75 g (3 oz) butter
salt
175 g (6 oz) flour
1 medium sized egg yolk
1 tablespoon cold water
a 20 cm (8 inch) flan tin with loose base

Serves 6–8

100 g (4 oz) butter
salt
225 g (8 oz) flour
1 large egg yolk
1 tablespoon cold water
a 25 cm (10 inch) flan tin with loose base

Drop the butter into a warmed bowl and soften it to a cream with a wooden spoon. Add a pinch of salt to the flour and sift it into a mound in a mixing bowl. Make a well in the centre and drop in the butter, egg yolk, another pinch of salt and the cold water. Mix these last ingredients together with a wooden spoon, holding the bowl with the other hand. When combined, gather in the flour with the fingers, turning the bowl round at the same time, adding a second tablespoon of cold water if necessary, blending in the flour until a soft ball is formed. Wrap in greaseproof paper and refrigerate for 30 minutes. Roll out the pastry, fold into four and roll out again. Fold a second time and refrigerate for 30 minutes before use.

Croustade aux champignons
(Mushroom Tart)
Serves 4 as a main course,
6 as a first course

pâte brisée for 4–6 (see page 47)
450 g (1 lb) button mushrooms
125 g (5 oz) butter
juice 1 lemon
salt, black pepper
1 teaspoon flour
150 ml ($\frac{1}{4}$ pint) chicken *bouillon*
2 small egg yolks
2 tablespoons double cream
a 20 cm (8 inch) flan tin with loose base

Remove the pastry from the refrigerator 15 minutes before rolling out. Heat the oven to 200° C, 400° F, Gas 6. Cover a baking sheet with foil and place in oven. Lightly butter the flan tin and sprinkle with flour.

Roll out the pastry and line the tin, trimming off the edges with a sharp knife. Prick the bottom with a fork and fill with dried beans. Place on the baking sheet and bake for 15 minutes, remove the beans, reduce the heat to 190°C, 375°F, Gas 5, and bake for a further 20 minutes. Cover lightly with foil if the pastry shows signs of colouring too deeply. It should be biscuit colour when baked. Cool for a few minutes, remove the rim and place the pastry on a wire tray.

Meanwhile wipe the mushrooms with a damp cloth and trim the stalks. Melt 100 g (4 oz) butter in a wide-based pan over low heat, add the lemon juice and throw in the mushrooms, salt lightly, cover and leave to render their juice.

In another pan melt remaining butter, work in the flour with a wooden spoon and when foaming, but not coloured, draw the pan from the heat and beat in the *bouillon* with a hand whisk.

Drain the mushrooms when tender, add their juice to the *bouillon* mixture, whisk until

incorporated and return the pan to the heat. Simmer for 10 minutes, stirring frequently. Season with pepper and add more salt if necessary. Beat the egg yolks into the cream in a small bowl. Remove the pan from the heat, add a tablespoon of the sauce to the cream, stir well and return it to the pan. Heat very gently without boiling, stirring constantly, until very thick. Mix in the mushrooms and allow to cool a little. Pour into the pastry case and serve warm.

Croustade florentine
(Beef, Pork and Spinach Tart)
Serves 4 as a main course,
6 as a first course

pâte brisée for 4–6 (see page 47)
750 g (1$\frac{1}{2}$ lb) fresh spinach or 350 g (12 oz) frozen spinach
1 medium sized onion
50 g (2 oz) Parmesan cheese
100 g (4 oz) butter
2 tablespoons olive oil
175 g (6 oz) lean minced beef
175 g (6 oz) lean minced pork
salt, black pepper
1 tablespoon flour
2 tablespoons double cream
a 23 cm (9 inch) flan tin with loose base

Remove the pastry from the refrigerator 30 minutes before rolling out. Lightly butter the flan tin and sprinkle with flour.

If using fresh spinach wash in several changes of cold water, remove the centre rib and cook in a dry pan with just the water clinging to the leaves. Cook over medium heat for 5 minutes. Drain and leave to cool. If using frozen spinach drop the block into a dry pan and leave over low heat until thawed, increase the heat and boil for 5 minutes. Drain and leave to cool. Squeeze the spinach between the palms to remove all moisture and chop coarsely.

Peel and chop the onion. Grate the cheese. Melt 25 g (1 oz) butter with the oil in a heavy frying pan and when foaming add the onion and cook over low heat until soft, stirring frequently to avoid browning. Add the beef and pork, season well and mix thoroughly. Cook for 10 minutes, stirring occasionally. Sprinkle with the flour and Parmesan, stir well and continue cooking until the mixture is dry. Turn out of the frying pan on to a plate and leave to cool.

Heat oven to 200°C, 400°F, Gas 6. Cover a baking sheet with foil and place in oven. Wipe out the frying pan with kitchen paper, melt 50 g (2 oz) butter and when foaming add the spinach and stir over low heat until dry, pour in the cream, mix well and set aside. Roll out the pastry and line the tin, trim the edges with a sharp knife and prick the bottom with a fork. Cover with half of the meat mixture, spread the spinach and cream on top and cover with the rest of the meat. Cut the remainder of the butter into little flecks and dot them over the surface.

Bake for 35 to 40 minutes, remove rim of flan tin and serve immediately.

In winter time the mountain farms produce snacks that send up the body temperature in a trice and none more quickly than this rarebit.

Croûtes au kirsch
(Kirsch and Ham Rarebit)
Serves 6

225 g (8 oz) gruyère cheese
3 tablespoons double cream
7 large eggs
pepper, nutmeg
6 slices bread (cut 2 cm [¾ inch] thick)
100 g (4 oz) butter
4 tablespoons oil
1 tablespoon vinegar
6 tablespoons kirsch
6 thin slices boiled ham

Grate the cheese. Beat the cream, grated cheese and 1 egg together, season with pepper and grated nutmeg and set aside. Heat the grill at medium-high temperature.

Remove the crusts from the bread. Melt 25 g (1 oz) butter and 1 tablespoon oil in a large frying pan and colour the bread golden on both sides, adding more butter and oil as required. Meanwhile start poaching the eggs in a large panful of salted water to which the vinegar has been added. Take care to poach the eggs *very lightly*. As the bread colours take each slice out of the pan, place it in a small flameproof dish, sprinkle with kirsch and cover with a slice of ham. Drain the eggs well and place them on the ham. Beat the cheese mixture again and pour it over the eggs.

Increase the grill heat to maximum and place the eggs under it. Leave just long enough for the cheese to melt.

Serve without delay with a liqueurglass of kirsch for each person.

Rabelais is known to have relished a *fouace*, the savoury tart made with curd cheese in the farmhouses of the Deux-Sèvres. The rounded dark-brown surface of the *fouace* is distinctive and they are still sold in country markets.

The cheese used, when not home-made, must be bought loose from the delicatessen counter. The processed variety sold in cartons is not suitable for this recipe.

La fouace aux herbes
(Curd Cheese and Herb Tart)
Serves 4 as a main course,
6 as a first course

pâte brisée for 4–6 (see page 47)
2 bunches spring onions
3 medium sized eggs
salt, black pepper
25 g (1 oz) butter
8 large sorrel leaves or 1 tablespoon chopped
    tarragon
2 tablespoons chopped parsley
2 tablespoons chopped chives
150 g (5 oz) curd cheese
1 tablespoon milk (optional)
a 20 cm (8 inch) flan tin with loose base

Remove the pastry from the refrigerator 15 minutes before rolling out. Trim the spring onions, removing the roots but retaining all edible green leaves. Separate the eggs. Beat the egg whites to a stiff peak with a pinch of salt and set aside.

Lightly butter the flan tin and sprinkle with flour. Roll out the pastry, line the tin and trim the edges with a sharp knife. Do not chill. Heat the oven to 190°C, 375°F, Gas 5. Cover a baking sheet with foil and place in oven.

Cut the spring onions into small pieces, green leaves included. Melt the butter in a frying pan and when foaming add the onions and cook slowly until soft, add the sorrel cut into strips (if used) and stir until melted. Add the rest of the herbs, season well and mix together, adding a little more butter if the mixture seems dry. Leave to cool. Spread over the bottom of the pastry case. Beat the egg yolks into the curd cheese and season highly. If the mixture is stiff add milk, then beat until it is the consistency of thick cream. Beat the egg whites again until very stiff and using a wooden spatula fold into the cheese mixture with an up-and-over movement so that they enfold the mixture and are not beaten or stirred in. Pour into the pastry case and bake for 35 minutes until well risen and dark brown on top. Allow to cool a little, remove rim of flan tin and serve warm or cold with a green salad.

Savouries

French grape-farmers have various little gastronomic treats to help them savour the quality of their wines. One of the simplest and best is *les lèches au fromage*. In the dialect of the Beaujolais area a *lèche* is a slice of country bread.

Lèches au fromage
(Cheese and Walnut Tidbits)

Equal quantities of grated Emmenthal cheese and finely chopped walnuts are mixed together and spread thickly on lightly buttered bread which is then cut into wide strips. Use light rye or wholemeal bread. In either case it should be two days old so that it is firm and not crumbly.

For more important occasions warm tidbits are served, such as:

Gougères bourguignonnes
(Hot Cheese Tidbits)
Serves 6

200 g (7 oz) flour
150 g (5 oz) gruyère cheese
100 g (4 oz) butter
200 ml (7 fl oz) water
¼ teaspoon salt
black pepper
5 medium sized eggs
1 small egg
1 tablespoon cold water

Sift the flour on to a folded paper and set aside.

Cut 100 g (4 oz) of the cheese into very fine slivers and finely dice the remainder.

Cut the butter into pieces and put it into a large saucepan with the water and salt. Place over medium heat and when the water boils stir until the butter is melted. Season with pepper, draw the pan from the heat and add the flour all at once. Work it in with a wooden spatula until smooth. Replace the pan over the heat, increase the heat a little and work the paste very thoroughly until it leaves the sides and base of the pan quite clean. Take the pan from the heat and add the medium sized eggs one at a time, working the paste vigorously between each addition. Add the slivers of cheese at the same time little by little, and beat until melted.

Heat the oven to 220°C, 425°F, Gas 7.

Beat the small egg with the cold water and set aside. Butter a baking sheet and drop the cheese mixture on to it, a heaped tablespoonful at a time, well spaced out. Brush with beaten egg, place a few dice of cheese on top and bake for 20 minutes. Remove from the oven, cool for 5 minutes and serve warm.

For tasting their sweet Anjou wines some growers serve an unusual tidbit, which by sharp contrast, brings out the sweet flavour of the grape as no other savoury mouthful can do. For this, it is essential for all ingredients to be of first class quality.

Petites bouchées de gruyère
(Gruyère Tidbits)
Makes about 15

225 g (8 oz) fresh Swiss gruyère or Emmenthal cheese
75 g (3 oz) unsalted butter
allspice

Cut the cheese into rectangles about 2.5 cm (1 inch) × 7 cm (2½ inches), 5 mm (¼ inch) thick. Spread liberally with butter. Grind a little allspice over the surface. Arrange on a large decorative plate like the spokes of a wheel and serve garnished with sprigs of parsley.

Eggs

Old wives tell their tales the world over, but when a recipe is involved they are taken seriously. It would seem that the following dish became popular during the French Revolution of 1789.

A band of revolutionaries named *les Chouans* (after a certain Jean Chouan who led them), roamed through Vendée on the run. They were fed willingly, if frugally, by the peasants who also took them in and hid them when necessary. Food in those times was scarce but two eggs, an onion and a glass of wine were always to be begged, borrowed, or stolen in a good cause. They still make a delicious and satisfying meal when bolstered up with plenty of thick-crusted country bread.

Oeufs à la Chouan
(Eggs in Red Wine Sauce)
Serves 4

1 large onion or 12 shallots
1 clove garlic
50 g (2 oz) butter
300 ml (½ pint) red wine
1 small sprig thyme
1 bay leaf
2 stalks parsley
salt, black pepper, nutmeg
8 large eggs

Peel the onion and garlic and chop finely together. Melt the butter in a large frying pan over medium heat and when foaming add the onion mixture. Reduce the heat to low and cook slowly until soft and transparent, without colouring. Stir frequently, add the wine, the herbs tied together, salt, pepper and a large pinch of grated nutmeg. When simmering slowly, leave to reduce a little.

Meanwhile break the eggs into wetted saucers and slide them into the pan. Flip the sauce over the yolks until they are veiled and the whites just set. Remove the herbs. Put a pinch of salt and a twist of ground pepper in the centre of each yolk and serve the eggs immediately on a hot plate with the sauce poured round them.

Any dish served in a good sauce is popular with French country people. None of it is wasted with their well-crusted bread to hand.

Oeufs à la châtelaine
(Eggs in Onion and Chestnut Sauce)
Serves 6

18 chestnuts (fresh or canned in water)
1 large onion
60 g (2½ oz) butter
1 tablespoon flour
600 ml (1 pint) hot milk
salt, white and black pepper, paprika
6 canned artichoke hearts
2 tablespoons wine vinegar
600 ml (1 pint) salted water
6 large eggs
4 tablespoons cream

If using fresh chestnuts, heat the oven to 240°C, 475°F, Gas 9. Slit the skin on the rounded side. Place them in a baking tin in one layer, add 1 cm (½ inch) boiling water, put the tin in the oven and bake for about 10 minutes until the skins burst and the nuts are soft inside. Remove both skins and crumble the nuts into large pieces. If using tinned chestnuts, drain and dry them well. Crumble the nuts into large pieces.

Peel and slice the onion and cook until soft in 25 g (1 oz) butter, drain and set aside. Melt another 25 g (1 oz) butter in a saucepan over medium heat and when foaming work in the flour. Gradually beat in the milk, stirring constantly. Season well with salt, white and black pepper, add the onion and cook slowly until thick and bubbling. Reduce the heat to low and simmer for about 7 minutes, stirring constantly. Draw the pan from the heat, cover the contents closely with a buttered paper to prevent a skin forming, and set aside.

Drain the artichoke hearts and pat dry with kitchen paper. Melt the remaining butter in a large frying pan and when foaming sauté the hearts until very hot. Drain and place in a buttered *gratin* dish. Season, cover and keep hot in the oven.

Add the vinegar to the salted water and bring to boiling point over low heat. Break the eggs into wetted saucers and slide them into the pan. Poach for about 3 minutes until just set, then remove from the pan with a fish slice and keep hot in a bowl of warm water. Reheat the sauce, whisk again, add the cream and crumbled chestnuts. Place one egg on each artichoke heart, pour the sauce over them, sprinkle with paprika and serve immediately with hot dry toast.

Oeufs aux poivrons
(Eggs in Green Pepper and Tomato Sauce)
Serves 4

1 large green pepper
1 large red pepper
about 4 tablespoons olive oil
450 g (1 lb) large tomatoes
2 medium sized onions
1 clove garlic
salt, black pepper, cayenne
1 bay leaf
2 sprigs thyme
4 large eggs

Heat the grill to medium temperature.

Remove the stem end of the peppers, cut into halves, remove seeds and white intersections. Place the halves on the cutting board and press down to flatten as much as possible. Brush with oil and place under the grill. When the skin blisters put the peppers immediately into a large paper bag, close tightly and leave for 10 minutes. Then peel off the fine skin and cut the peppers into strips.

Meanwhile prick the tomatoes in several places, plunge them into boiling water for 1 minute and then into cold. Skin, cut into halves, remove the seeds with a teaspoon and chop the flesh roughly. Peel and roughly chop the onions and garlic. Heat 3 tablespoons olive oil in a *sauteuse* or large frying pan over low heat, add the peppers, onions and garlic and cook slowly until soft. Add the tomatoes, salt, pepper, a generous pinch of cayenne, the crumbled bay leaf and finely rubbed thyme. Cook slowly, uncovered, until thick, stirring occasionally.

Pour the mixture into a metal *gratin* dish, make 4 small hollows with the back of a spoon and break an egg into each one. Place over low heat, cover with a lid and simmer until the eggs are just set. Sprinkle each yolk with salt and pepper and serve immediately.

If no metal dish is available bake in the oven at 180°C, 350°F, Gas 4, covered with foil.

The French, according to Thomas Moore, had in the 18th century already found 686 ways to dress eggs and this he found endearing. He did not however mention the country people's gift for naming them.

What could be more apt than *Eggs in Overcoats* to describe soft-baked eggs covered by a thick mousse flavoured with anchovies and capers.

Oeufs en surtout
(Eggs with Anchovies and Capers)
Serves 4

2 teaspoons capers
6 anchovy fillets
2 tablespoons chopped parsley
2 tablespoons chopped chives or spring onions
6 large eggs
salt, black pepper, nutmeg
15 g (½ oz) butter

Heat the oven to 180°C, 350°F, Gas 4, and place on the middle shelf 4 shallow ovenproof dishes the size of saucers.

Chop the capers and anchovy fillets together coarsely, add the parsley and chives or spring onions and chop finely. Separate 2 of the eggs and mix the anchovy mixture with the 2 yolks. Season with very little salt, plenty of pepper and a generous pinch of grated nutmeg. Beat well and set aside. Beat the whites to a soft peak.

Break the remaining eggs into wetted saucers, butter the hot dishes, slide 1 egg into each and season the yolks. Fold the anchovy mixture into the egg whites and quickly divide it between the 4 dishes to cover the eggs and touch the sides of the dish. Bake for exactly 10 minutes, no more, and serve without delay.

Omelette au thon mariné
(Tuna Omelette)
Serves 4 as a main course,
6 as a first course

2 teaspoons soft butter
1 teaspoon finely chopped parsley
4 soft herring roes
½ clove garlic
salt, black pepper
50 g (2 oz) canned tuna
40 g (1½ oz) butter
6 large eggs
juice ½ lemon

Mix the soft butter with the parsley, using a flexible knife. Chill. When firm, cut into small pieces.

Blanch the roes in boiling salted water for 3 minutes. Drain and set aside. Peel the garlic and crush to a paste with a pinch of salt, using the flat side of a knife blade.

Drain the tuna and shred finely. Put the roes, garlic and tuna into a saucepan with 25 g (1 oz) butter, cut into small pieces. Place over low heat and mix well. Break the eggs into a small bowl, season and mix well with a fork. As soon as the butter in the pan melts, remove from the heat, pour in the eggs and stir thoroughly.

Heat a large heavy iron frying pan over a medium temperature, dry, for a few moments. Add remaining butter and when it froths swirl it round the pan to coat the surface. Pour in the egg mixture, draw it in from sides to centre with a spatula to allow the liquid to run to the sides, and loosen the edges as they set. While the omelette is still liquid on the surface fold it over and slide it on to a heated serving dish in which half the pieces of parsley butter have been placed. Dot with the remaining parsley butter, sprinkle with lemon juice and serve immediately.

Oeufs aux herbes
(Eggs with Fresh Herbs)
Serves 4

4 large eggs
1 tablespoon water
salt, black pepper
1 handful each parsley, chives, tarragon
25 g (1 oz) butter

Heat the grill at medium heat. Break the eggs into a small bowl, add the water, salt and pepper. Mix well with a fork (do not beat), and set aside.

Wash the herbs under running water and shake out excess moisture. Dry well on kitchen paper and pick off the leaves from the stalks of parsley and tarragon, discarding stalks. Cut the chives into short lengths and chop all the herbs together in a cup with a pair of sharp scissors. Mix into the stirred eggs. Cut the butter into little pieces.

Put an 18 cm (7 inch) diameter iron frying pan, dry, over gentle heat. When the pan is quite hot drop in half the butter, swirl it round the pan and as it starts to colour pour in the egg and herb mixture. Scatter the rest of the butter on top in little flecks and move the mixture around drawing sides to centre to allow the liquid to flow to the sides again. As soon as the edges are set, loosen them all round with a palette knife and put the pan under the grill to lightly set the surface. The trick is to brown the underside to the golden stage, set the top and leave the centre creamy. Loosen all round again, set a plate on top of the pan and invert quickly, turning out the *galette* golden side uppermost. When cool, chill slightly before cutting into 4 portions.

Serve with a green salad.

Rice

Riz au blanc
(Boiled Rice)
Serves 4

225 g (8 oz) rice
1 teaspoon salt
1 thick slice lemon
25 g (1 oz) butter or 2 tablespoons olive oil
black pepper

Wash the rice under cold running water and leave to drain. Rub the inside rim of a very large pan with buttered paper to prevent boiling over and fill three-quarters full with boiling water. Add salt and lemon and when boiling rapidly, scatter the rice over the surface a little at a time so that the water does not stop boiling. Cook for exactly 10 minutes, then test. Meanwhile heat the oven to 170°C, 325°F, Gas 3. Put the butter or oil in a large shallow dish, and place dish in oven.

If rice is still hard between the teeth after 10 minutes, cook for a further 2 or 3 minutes, but 15 minutes is the longest it should cook if it is to remain firm. It should not be soft. Tip the contents of the pan into a colander and hold under cold running water for 3 or 4 minutes, turning the rice occasionally. Shake the colander and bang it on the draining board to expel as much water as possible.

Swirl the melted butter around the dish to coat the sides and empty the rice into it. Season well and spread out evenly with a fork. Place in the centre of the oven to dry slowly; turn the rice over occasionally and spread it out again each time. Test for seasoning and correct if necessary. When hot, dry and fluffy, serve immediately.

If not to be served immediately, cover lightly with a piece of buttered foil and leave on the lowest shelf of the oven.

The dish can be garnished with flecks of butter and sprinkled with grated Parmesan cheese to serve with some dishes.

Farmhouse larders are famous for the amount of leftovers they can collect, probably because such vast amounts of food are prepared in the first place. But Frenchwomen have a genius for using leftovers, and they have an especially delicious recipe for making the most of any cooked rice. In fact, a double quantity of rice is often prepared deliberately so that *boules de riz* can be made another day.

Boules de riz
(Stuffed Rice Balls)
Serves 4

150 g (5 oz) gruyère cheese (cut in one slice
    1 cm [$\frac{1}{2}$ inch] thick)
2 medium sized eggs
salt, black pepper
325 g (11 oz) cold cooked seasoned rice
6–7 tablespoons fine dry breadcrumbs
oil for deep frying

Cut the cheese into 1 cm ($\frac{1}{2}$ inch) cubes and set aside.

Beat the eggs with a fork and season well. Stir in the rice gently in order not to mash it. Scoop up a tablespoon of rice, push a cube of cheese into the centre and place another tablespoon of rice on top. Shape into a ball between the two spoons or shape between wetted palms. Roll in crumbs and place on greaseproof paper. Refrigerate for 30 minutes. Meanwhile heat the oil to 190°C, 375°F, and heat the oven to 130°C, 250°F, Gas $\frac{1}{2}$.

Line a baking sheet with absorbent kitchen paper and place it in the oven. Fry the balls 4 at a time for about 5 minutes, until golden brown. Drain on the paper in the oven and serve very hot. When cooked they can be kept hot for 10 minutes in the oven if necessary.

Serve with a green salad.

In the grape-growing areas wine is used for cooking as a matter of course, and the wine producer's wife has a selection to choose from. She makes rice into a very special dish by cooking it with white wine.

Riz au vin
(Rice in White Wine)
Serves 4

1 large onion
1 large carrot
50 g (2 oz) butter
225 g (8 oz) rice
salt, black pepper
$\frac{1}{2}$ teaspoon dried marjoram
150 ml ($\frac{1}{4}$ pint) *bouillon*
150 ml ($\frac{1}{4}$ pint) dry white wine
about 50 g (2 oz) grated Parmesan cheese

Peel and chop the onion medium-fine. Peel the carrot, slice finely and chop coarsely. Melt the butter in a *sauteuse* or large frying pan over medium heat and when foaming sauté the onion and carrot until golden brown, stirring frequently to prevent burning. Add the rice and stir well to coat with butter, season and stir in the marjoram, *bouillon* and wine. Cover, reduce the heat and simmer until the liquid is absorbed. If this happens before the rice is cooked, add 1 or 2 tablespoons hot water. The rice is cooked when a grain is still slightly crisp when bitten. Depending on the quality of the rice this should take about 15 minutes. Correct the seasoning if necessary, empty the rice into a well-heated bowl and sprinkle with grated Parmesan cheese.

Serve very hot as an accompaniment to grilled or roasted meats.

Noodles

Noodles, rice and other farinaceous dishes are not the prerogative of the Italians. Provençal cooks make their own noodles and have their own different ways of serving them. In Provençal dialect this delicious home-made product is known as *li taiarin*.

The process of rolling and cutting the paste has been made easy by the importation into England of a simple, inexpensive machine which is now readily available in kitchen equipment shops. But the country people's method of cutting the paste by hand, described below, gives good results with little trouble.

Li taiarin
(Provençal Home-made Noodles)
Serves 4 as a main course,
6 as a first course

saffron, salt
1 tablespoon warm water
450 g (1 lb) unbleached white flour
   (obtainable at health food shops)
3 medium sized eggs
1 medium sized egg yolk

Put a pinch of saffron to soak in the warm water. Sift the flour into a mound in a mixing bowl and make a well in the centre. Beat the eggs, egg yolk and a pinch of salt together in a small bowl and pour them gradually into the well, mixing them into the flour with a wooden spoon until the paste becomes crumbly. Moisten the crumbs with the strained saffron water and gather them into a ball with the fingers. Divide the dough into 2 halves and knead each one on the lightly floured board, adding extra flour if it sticks. Shaping it into a long roll, fold it over on to itself and press it down with the heel of the hand before knead-ing, shaping and folding over again. Work each ball for 5 minutes, then work them together in the same way for 5 minutes until the dough is quite smooth. Wrap in a cloth and set aside for 10 minutes.

Cut off half of the dough, keeping the rest wrapped up. Flour the board, shape the dough into an oblong about 2.5 cm (1 inch) thick, and then roll out with a floured rolling pin. Starting at the end nearest to you, roll away from you to within 1 cm (½ inch) of the far edge. Turn the dough a quarter turn to the right and roll again in the same way across the width. Repeat rolling and turning until the dough is paper thin. If it sticks lift it up carefully and dust lightly with flour. When rolled, dust lightly with flour and set aside on greaseproof paper covered with a clean cloth. Repeat with the remainder of the dough.

Taking the first half, dust again with flour and holding the edge of the long side with the fingers, roll it to the centre and roll the other side inwards to meet it. Cut across with a sharp knife into 5 mm (¼ inch) wide strips, unfold them and spread out on a floured cloth. Sprinkle with flour and leave to dry for 30 minutes before use. Repeat with the remainder of the rolled dough.

If the noodles are not to be cooked immediately put them into a large paper bag and store in the refrigerator.

There are some very appetising and unusual sauces to serve with noodles, many of which include Parmesan and gruyère cheese. When bought in the piece and grated as required they both have a much fuller flavour than when bought ready grated. Parmesan should be well wrapped in greaseproof paper and stored in the refrigerator. It will keep indefinitely in this way and the harder and drier it becomes the better.

A finely sliced potato cooked with noodles helps them absorb the cheese or other sauce.

Li taiarin à la crème
(Noodles with Cream and Cheese)
Serves 4 as a main course,
6 as a first course

1 potato
100 g (4 oz) Parmesan cheese
100 g (4 oz) butter
4 tablespoons double cream
450 g (1 lb) noodles (see page 57)
salt, black pepper

Finely slice the potato. Grate the cheese and set aside. Heat the oven to 130°C, 250°F, Gas ½ and place a large earthenware serving bowl inside. Soften the butter a little, work to a cream with a fork and beat in the cream and grated cheese gradually. Set aside.

Butter the rim of a large pan to prevent boiling over, fill it nearly full with boiling water, add the potato slices, place over medium-high heat and when boiling fast, drop in the noodles, stir to prevent them sticking to the bottom and boil for exactly 7 minutes. Test; they should be slightly firm when bitten into, not soft. Drain through a colander, empty into the hot bowl and season well. Pour the cream mixture over the noodles, turning them over and over quickly with a wooden spoon and fork until well coated.

Serve immediately on hot plates.

Li taiarin au jambon
(Noodles with Ham, Chicken and Cheese)
Serves 4 as a main course,
6 as a first course

75 g (3 oz) gruyère cheese
100 g (4 oz) lean boiled ham (cut thick)
100 g (4 oz) button mushrooms
2 tablespoons lemon juice
100 g (4 oz) cold cooked chicken (white meat only)
450 g (1 lb) noodles (see page 57)
1 potato
50 g (2 oz) butter
1 tablespoon flour
salt, black pepper
450 ml (16 fl oz) milk

Grate the cheese and set aside. Remove any fat from the ham and cut the lean into narrow strips. Wipe the mushrooms with a damp cloth, trim the stalks, finely slice and turn them in lemon juice immediately to prevent discolouration. Cut the chicken meat into fine slivers and set aside.

Cook the noodles with the potato as described in previous recipe, but keep them slightly under-cooked. Drain well and keep hot over a pan of simmering water.

Meanwhile melt 25 g (1 oz) butter in a large wide-based pan and when foaming work in the flour with a wooden spoon. Season lightly with salt and generously with pepper and draw the pan from the heat. Pour in the milk all at once and beat briskly with a wire whisk to eliminate lumps. When smooth, return the pan to medium heat and, stirring constantly, simmer for 5 minutes after boiling point is reached.

Heat the grill at maximum temperature and have ready a heated and buttered *gratin* dish. Melt the remaining butter. Add the ham, mushrooms and chicken to the sauce and cook together for a further 5 minutes, stirring frequently. Then add the drained noodles, stir thoroughly to incorporate them, sprinkle with half the cheese, draw the pan from the heat and mix cheese in thoroughly. Pour into the *gratin* dish, scatter the remainder of the cheese on top and pour the melted butter evenly over the surface. Place under the grill for 5 minutes until brown and crusted and serve immediately.

The most popular way of serving noodles in Provence is with *pestou*, a thick cream of garlic, fresh basil, Parmesan cheese and olive oil. Basil grows luxuriantly in every Mediterranean garden and is an important ingredient of many country recipes of that region. It can be grown easily in an English garden or in a pot on a sunny window sill (see page 10).

Pestou
(Garlic and Basil Dressing)

100 g (4 oz) Parmesan cheese
4 cloves garlic
1 tablespoon chopped basil
5–6 tablespoons olive oil

Grate the cheese and set it aside. Peel and roughly chop the garlic cloves, then crush and pound them in a mortar with the basil until a thick purée is formed. Continue pounding while adding the cheese and then beat in the oil drop by drop as for mayonnaise. Continue beating until a thick green cream is obtained.

To serve *pestou* with noodles, cook and drain noodles as advised on page 58, turn them into a heated earthenware bowl, pour the *pestou* over and mix thoroughly with a large wooden spoon and fork. Serve immediately with grated Parmesan handed separately.

To make the *pestou* go further, parsley and tomatoes are sometimes added. Finely chop the leaves of a small handful of parsley and work it into the *pestou* with the basil. Skin 2 large Mediterranean tomatoes (or 4 large domestic tomatoes), remove the seeds, cut the flesh into pieces and pass them through a vegetable mill or *mouli-légumes*; add the tomato purée to the *pestou* with the cheese.

Chapter Five

SALADS

French country salads, like country appetites, are robust. Several of the following recipes, although usually served as a first course, make an excellent salad lunch when served with crisp bread and a glass of wine.

Salade de betteraves à cru
(Raw Beetroot Salad)
Serves 6 as a first course

3 teaspoons tarragon-flavoured wine vinegar
150 ml ($\frac{1}{4}$ pint) double cream
salt, black pepper
1 tablespoon chopped tarragon
350 g (12 oz) raw beetroot

Mix the tarragon vinegar into the cream, season with salt and pepper and stir in the chopped tarragon. Test for seasoning and add a few more drops of vinegar if required. Peel the beetroot and grate it coarsely into the dressing. Mix well and allow to stand for 1 hour before serving.

Céleri en salade
(Celery and Cheese Salad)
Serves 4 as a lunch dish,
6 as a first course

2 heads of celery
salt, black pepper
100 g (4 oz) walnut halves
100 g (4 oz) Roquefort or Stilton cheese
1 tablespoon brandy
4 tablespoons *vinaigrette* (see following recipe)

Trim and wash the heads of celery. Discard all tough outside leaves, dry the celery well and chop into small pieces, tender green leaves included. Place in the salad bowl and season lightly with salt and pepper. Chop the nuts coarsely and add to the celery. Place in the refrigerator until required.

Crumble the cheese into a small bowl, crush with a fork and work in the brandy until the cheese is soft. Now mix in the *vinaigrette* little by little, beating constantly until thoroughly blended.

To serve, pour the sauce over the celery and nuts, mix well and serve immediately.

Vinaigrette
(French Dressing)

1 tablespoon wine vinegar (tarragon or mustard-flavoured or plain)
$\frac{1}{2}$ teaspoon salt
black pepper
3 tablespoons olive oil

Pour the vinegar into a small bowl, add the salt and stir until it dissolves. (If the oil is added before the salt, the salt will not dissolve.) Season with pepper and beat in the oil gradually until the dressing is thick and cloudy. Whatever the quantity of dressing required always use 1 part wine vinegar to 3 parts oil.

Olive oil is used when making a plain dressing but when some flavouring is added such as chopped herbs, onions, capers or French mustard, corn oil may be used instead.

Vinaigrette can be used on all green salads.

Salade de chicorée au gruyère
(Curly Endive and Cheese Salad)
Serves 4

1 curly endive
50 g (2 oz) gruyère cheese
1 piece breadcrust
1 clove garlic
4 tablespoons *vinaigrette* (see page 61)

Cut a slice from the root end of the endive.

Pour 1 cm ($\frac{1}{2}$ inch) cold water into the bottom of a large bowl and place the endive in the bowl root end down. Leave in a cool dark place for at least 1 hour. This will refresh the endive and make the wilted leaves firm again.

Plunge the endive up and down head first in a bowl of cold water, changing the water until it is quite clean. Shake as dry as possible, pick off all leaves, discarding those that are damaged, and swing the rest dry in a wire basket or clean kitchen towel. Pat dry with a cloth. Unless the salad leaves are quite dry the salad will not be crisp. Store in a tightly closed plastic bag in the refrigerator until required.

Cut the cheese into thick matchlike strips. Break the endive leaves into pieces. Rub the inside of the salad bowl, and the breadcrust, with the cut clove of garlic, then discard the clove. Beat the *vinaigrette* until cloudy and pour into the bowl, add the salad and the crust and turn all over carefully with a wooden spoon and fork until the leaves are coated with dressing. Add the cheese, turn the salad again and serve immediately. The *chapon* or garlic-flavoured crust is regarded as a tidbit by garlic addicts.

If the salad is not to be served at once, heap the undressed salad leaves lightly in the bowl over the crossed salad servers and dressing and place in the refrigerator. When ready to serve toss thoroughly, add the cheese and toss again before serving.

Salade de haricots verts aux échalotes
(Green Bean and Shallot Salad)
Serves 4

450 g (1 lb) small green beans
1 shallot
2–3 teaspoons lemon juice
3 tablespoons double cream
salt, black pepper
1 tablespoon chopped chervil or parsley

Top and tail the beans and cook whole in boiling salted water until only just tender. They must remain slightly crisp.

Meanwhile peel the shallot and chop very finely. Beat 2 teaspoons lemon juice into the cream, season with salt and pepper and stir in the chopped chervil or parsley and shallot. Drain the beans thoroughly and add to the dressing while still hot. Turn them over carefully to coat well. Test for seasoning and add more salt and lemon juice if necessary. Serve when cold.

Salade de pommes de terre chaude
(Hot Potato and Sausage Salad)
Serves 4 as a lunch or supper dish, 6 as a first course

1.2 kg (2$\frac{1}{2}$ lb) red-skinned potatoes
225 g (8 oz) smoked sausage
1 tablespoon corn oil
150 ml ($\frac{1}{4}$ pint) dry white wine
salt, black pepper
6 tablespoons *vinaigrette* (see page 61)
2 tablespoons chopped chives

Scrub the potatoes and boil in their skins until just tender. Boil slowly to prevent the skin bursting, and do not overcook.

Meanwhile cut the sausage into thick rings and sauté in hot oil until golden. Drain on kitchen paper and keep hot.

Pour the wine into a large heated bowl and as each potato is peeled turn it in the wine. Then cut the potatoes into thick slices, season well and pour the *vinaigrette* over them. Turn the slices over to coat with dressing, cover and place the bowl over a pan of simmering water. Add the chives to the sausage rings and mix them lightly into the potatoes. Test for seasoning and correct if necessary. Serve hot with the same wine as that used in the recipe.

In very early spring when the tender young dandelions first appear (see page 11), country people look upon them as a delicacy and as a tonic. This is how they serve them on Ash Wednesday in the villages of the Deux-Sèvres.

Salade de pissenlits de Souché
(Souché Dandelion and Bacon Salad)
Serves 4

4 handfuls tender young dandelions
100 g (4 oz) streaky bacon (in one piece)
2 hard-boiled eggs (hot)
salt, black pepper
about 1 tablespoon red wine vinegar

Trim the root of the dandelions, but retain enough root to hold the leaves together. Refresh as for endive on facing page, drain well and dry. Set aside until required.

Remove the rind from the bacon and cut the meat into small dice. Place in a heavy iron frying pan over low heat and cook until the fat is rendered and the bacon crisp and golden brown on all sides.

Meanwhile peel the eggs and heat a large salad bowl. Place the prepared dandelions in

the bowl, cover with slices of hot hard-boiled egg, season well, pour vinegar into the pan, work it into the bacon fat, pour bacon and vinegar mixture over the salad and turn salad over quickly before the bacon fat cools. Serve immediately.

Salade poitevine
(Poitou Rice and Mushroom Salad)
Serves 4 as a lunch dish,
6 as a first course

6–8 tablespoons cold cooked rice (see page 55)
salt, black pepper
6 tablespoons *vinaigrette* (see page 61)
100 g (4 oz) button mushrooms
about 2 teaspoons lemon juice
4 firm tomatoes
1 small onion
1 tablespoon chopped tarragon or chives

Put the rice into a large salad bowl and sprinkle with salt and pepper. It must be well seasoned. Pour half the *vinaigrette* over it and mix thoroughly.

Wipe the mushrooms with a damp cloth and trim the stalk end. Cut into halves, stalk included. Pour about 1 cm ($\frac{1}{2}$ inch) cold water into a large saucepan, add salt and 1 teaspoon lemon juice. Add the mushrooms in one layer and place over low heat. When boiling point is reached, cover and simmer gently for 5 minutes. Drain and set aside.

Meanwhile prick the tomatoes in several places, plunge them into boiling water for 1 minute and then into cold. Skin, cut into halves, remove the seeds with a teaspoon and cut the flesh into thick pieces. Peel and chop the onion finely and toss the mushrooms, tomato and onion together, season well, mix with the remaining *vinaigrette* and then mix lightly into the rice with a wooden spoon and fork. Test for seasoning, correct if necessary and add a little lemon juice to sharpen the flavours. Sprinkle with chopped tarragon or chives and serve lightly chilled.

Chapter Six

FISH

The extensive coasts of France produce fish of infinite variety. Even the smallest towns, in their covered food halls and weekly street markets, offer an average of 30 varieties of freshly caught salt-water and fresh-water fish in all but the most rigorous seasons. The variety of shellfish is also considerable. In consequence the French repertory of fish recipes is extensive.

In the following chapter the recipes given will be found adaptable to any of the fish found, in more limited variety, in the English market.

The turbulent nature of the great rivers of France produces fish of superlative quality. The delicate flavour of eels, for example, is brought to perfection by such fast-flowing waters.

The finely flavoured rock-salmon or huss (which deserves far more notice than it gets) takes the place of eels very successfully. When cooked with fresh green herbs in the country manner, and served either hot or cold, it is a gourmet's dish.

Anguilles au vert
(Eels in Wine and Herb Sauce)
Serves 6

2 kg (4 lb) eels or rock-salmon
2 medium sized onions
3 branches celery
225 g (8 oz) sorrel
2 bunches watercress
50 g (2 oz) butter
750 ml (1¼ pints) dry white wine
4 tablespoons chopped parsley
4 tablespoons chopped chervil or dill
1 teaspoon chopped sage
1 teaspoon chopped mint
salt, black pepper
2–3 tablespoons lemon juice
200 ml (7 fl oz) double cream

If eels are used, have them skinned. Cut the fish into 5 cm (2 inch) lengths. Peel or trim the onions and celery and chop finely. Remove the centre rib from the sorrel, wash, shake dry, and cut into fine shreds with scissors. Wash the watercress, shake dry and pick off the leaves. Melt the butter in a large *sauteuse* or wide-based pan over moderate heat and when foaming add the pieces of fish and turn in the butter just long enough to make them firm. They must not colour. Add the wine, onions, celery, sorrel, watercress leaves and chopped herbs. Mix thoroughly, season well, cover and when boiling point is reached cook briskly for 10 to 15 minutes, until the fish is tender when pierced with a sharp-pointed knife.

Meanwhile stir the egg yolks into the cream and mix well before adding lemon juice to taste.

When the fish is cooked remove it with a slotted spoon (leaving the pan over low heat) and arrange on a heated serving dish, cover and keep hot.

Draw the pan from the heat, mix 2 or 3 tablespoons cooking liquid into the cream, stir well, pour back into the pan, and stirring constantly, reheat *slowly* until thick. On no account must the sauce boil. Correct the seasoning, add a little more lemon juice, if necessary, and pour the sauce over the fish. Serve immediately with new potatoes.

The remainder of the fish may be served cold. Arrange it on a clean serving dish with the sauce poured over it, cover and chill before serving.

A good *matelote* or fish stew is a favourite with fishermen since it can be used to include their whole catch of fresh-water fish: eels, carp, pike and even very small fish.

Matelote d'anguilles à la bourgeoise
(Mixed Fish in White Wine Sauce)
Serves 6

1.5–2 kg (3–4 lb) eels, carp, pike or other
   firm-fleshed fish
225 g (8 oz) button mushrooms
12 small onions (pickling size)
6 shallots
55 g (2¼ oz) butter
1 bay leaf
1 branch fennel
750 ml (1¼ pints) dry white wine
5 tablespoons double cream
1 teaspoon flour
2 medium sized egg yolks
salt, black pepper

Clean and scale the fish, remove head, tail and fins, wash quickly under cold running water and dry thoroughly. Cut into serving pieces and leave any small fish whole.

Wash and trim the mushrooms and dry thoroughly. Peel the small onions, peel and chop the shallots. Melt 50 g (2 oz) butter in a *sauteuse* or large saucepan over medium heat and when foaming add the whole onions and the chopped shallots. Stir with a wooden spatula to coat with butter, then add the pieces of fish and the herbs tied together. Add the wine, reduce the heat to low, and bring very gently to boiling point. As soon as this is reached, ignite the wine and baste the ingredients until the flames die down. A good wine will ignite immediately.

Slice the mushrooms into the pan and stir in 3 tablespoons cream. Cook for 10 to 15 minutes, over gentle heat so that the fish will not disintegrate. As soon as it is tender to the touch of a pointed knife remove the fish with a slotted spoon on to a heated serving dish, remove the small onions and place them around it. Cover and keep hot. Leave the pan over medium heat to reduce the liquid a little and mix the flour into the remaining butter with the blade of a knife. Mix the egg yolks with the rest of the cream and stir well.

Remove the herbs from the pan, drop in the butter mixture and beat thoroughly with a hand whisk until smooth. Increase the heat and simmer a little faster for 3 or 4 minutes to reduce the liquid. Draw the pan from the heat, add 2 tablespoons of the liquid to the cream and yolks, stirring it in gradually, then return this mixture to the pan. Stir until thickened and season to taste. Pour this sauce over the fish and serve immediately

The people of Picardy cook their fish not only with vegetables but also with ripe red gooseberries when in season. This excellent method is suitable for brill, or red or grey mullet.

Barbue picarde
(Brill with Gooseberries)
Serves 4

450 g (1 lb) red dessert gooseberries
4 large fillets of brill or mullet
50 g (2 oz) butter
8 mignonette or allspice corns
salt, black pepper
300 ml ($\frac{1}{2}$ pint) red wine
100 ml (4 fl oz) water
4–5 tablespoons *chapelure* (see right)

Heat the oven to 200°C, 400°F, Gas 6.

Top and tail the gooseberries, prick through with a large darning needle, place in one layer in a dish and pour boiling water over them. Leave until required. Wash the fish quickly under cold running water and dry thoroughly.

Butter a large shallow ovenproof dish thickly with a third of the butter and sprinkle with lightly crushed mignonette or allspice corns. Fold the fillets of brill over, place in the dish (mullet is best laid flat), season with salt and pepper and dot with the remaining butter.

Drain the gooseberries and place around the fish. Mix the wine with the water and pour down the sides of the dish. Cook in the oven for 20 minutes basting the fish twice. By this time the liquid will have reduced a little and the fish will be almost cooked (this depends on its thickness). Scatter the *chapelure* on top, return the dish to the oven and allow to brown and crust over. This should take about 10 minutes.

Serve immediately.

Chapelure
(Baked Breadcrumbs)

Chapelure is made with stale bread or crusts baked in the bottom of the oven when it is in use for other cooking. When quite hard, dry, and golden in colour, crush with a rolling pin until fine and store the crumbs in a screw-topped jar.

Cabillaud à la provençale
(Cod with Tomato and Herb Sauce)
Serves 6

4 shallots
225 g (8 oz) canned tomatoes
6 thick slices cod, hake, bass or other large, firm-fleshed fish
2 tablespoons olive oil
salt, black pepper
2 teaspoons *herbes de Provence* (see page 14) or mixed dried thyme, rosemary, basil, fennel
flour for coating
50 g (2 oz) butter
2 tablespoons corn oil

Peel and chop the shallots. Drain the tomatoes (reserving the juice for soup) and roughly chop. Wash the fish quickly under cold running water and dry thoroughly.

Heat the olive oil in a shallow pan, add the shallots, tomatoes, salt, pepper and herbs. Cook over brisk heat, stirring with a wooden spoon, until the moisture has evaporated and the mixture is soft and thick. Reduce the heat to low and keep hot until required.

Season the fish on both sides and dip in flour. Heat the butter with the corn oil in a large frying pan and when it froths cook the fish until golden, 4 to 5 minutes on each side.

Arrange on a heated serving dish, pour the reduced tomato sauce over the fish and serve immediately.

Cabillaud au vin blanc
(Cod in White Wine and Herb Sauce)
Serves 6

700 g (1½ lb) large tomatoes (preferably
    Mediterranean variety)
6 thick slices cod, hake, bass or other large,
    firm-fleshed fish
6 shallots or 4 small onions
60 g (2½ oz) butter
¼ teaspoon dried powdered thyme
1 bay leaf
1 sprig parsley
about 750 ml (1¼ pints) Chablis or Riesling
salt, black pepper
1 tablespoon each chopped parsley, tarragon,
    chervil
2 tablespoons double cream
1–2 teaspoons lemon juice

Heat the oven to 200°C, 400°F, Gas 6.

Prick the tomatoes in several places, plunge them into boiling water for 1 minute and then into cold. Skin, cut into halves, remove the seeds with a teaspoon and turn upside down to drain. Wash the fish quickly under cold running water and dry thoroughly.

Peel and finely chop the shallots or onions, melt the butter in a large frying pan over medium heat and when foaming cook them until transparent and soft. Pour into a large shallow oven dish with the butter and juices. Cut the tomato flesh into small pieces and spread in the dish. Sprinkle with the dried powdered thyme, the crumbled bay leaf and the sprig of parsley broken up. Arrange the fish on top in one layer and pour over enough wine to cover sparingly. Sprinkle with salt and pepper and place in the oven, centre shelf. In approximately 15 minutes, when the liquid is bubbling, turn off the heat and leave the fish inside for a further 5 minutes without opening the oven door.

Remove the dish from the oven, arrange the fish carefully on a heated serving dish, cover and keep hot.

Empty the cooking liquids and vegetables into a large saucepan and reduce by half over high heat. Strain through a fine sieve, pressing the vegetables against the sides with a wooden spoon to extract all the juices. Reheat until boiling. Draw the pan from the heat and stir in the fresh herbs. Add a tablespoon of this sauce to the cream, mix well and return it to the pan gradually, stirring it in. Correct the seasoning, add a few drops of lemon juice to sharpen the flavours, and pour over the fish.

Serve immediately with a dish of plain boiled potatoes.

La fouace aux herbes (see page 50).

French cockles are one of the free treats of the northern coasts of France, and the professional cockle gatherers have their own way of ridding these delicious shell-fish of the considerable amount of sand that they harbour.

Coques en salade
(Cockle Salad)
Serves 4

2.5 litres (4 pints) cockles
2 tablespoons water
herb mayonnaise (see following recipe)
2 hard-boiled eggs
sprigs parsley

Wash and scrub the cockles and wash again in several changes of water. Put them into a large pan with the water and place over a high heat. Shake the pan from time to time so that they all open, then strain through a colander reserving their liquor. When cold remove the cockles from their shells, hold under cold running water for 1 minute, turning the fish over occasionally, to remove the sand. Strain the pan liquor through a sieve lined with tissues into a shallow dish and place the cockles in it in one layer to marinate in their own juice and regain flavour. Leave until required.

Make the herb mayonnaise as instructed. Dry the cockles thoroughly and fold them into the mayonnaise. Shell the hard-boiled eggs and cut each one lengthways into 6 sections.

Turn the cockles and mayonnaise into a serving dish and garnish with the egg sections and sprigs of parsley.

Mayonnaise aux herbes
(Herb Mayonnaise)

1 large egg
½ teaspoon strong Dijon mustard
salt, black pepper
150 ml (¼ pint) olive or corn oil
1 teaspoon wine vinegar
1 teaspoon chopped chervil or parsley
1 tablespoon chopped chives

Put the ingredients together in a cool place several hours before making the mayonnaise. If they are all at the same temperature there is less likelihood of the sauce separating.

Separate the egg and slide the yolk into a large soup-plate, add the mustard, salt and pepper and beating meanwhile with a small hand whisk add the oil drop by drop, working it in very slowly over a wide circle. When thick, add the vinegar a drop at a time, beating constantly. If the mayonnaise should fail to thicken before adding the vinegar, work in a few drops of iced water, beating very vigorously meanwhile. Add a pinch of salt to the egg white and beat to a stiff peak. Fold it into the mayonnaise with the chopped herbs. Do not beat or stir.

Chill until required.

Poisson en daube (see page 75).

Farming folk are in favour of any recipes that use their continued supply of vegetables, just as they relish a good sauce into which they can dip their bread. This way of cooking whiting or thick fillets of any white fish provides them with both opportunities.

Merlans à la languedocienne
(Braised Whiting with Vegetables)
Serves 6

6 anchovy fillets
100 g (4 oz) + 1 tablespoon flour
3 tablespoons olive oil
salt, black pepper
150 ml ($\frac{1}{4}$ pint) + 3 tablespoons tepid water
2 lemons
1.5 kg (3 lb) fillets of whiting or thick fillets of any white fish
700 g ($1\frac{1}{2}$ lb) very ripe tomatoes
1 medium-large onion
1 carrot
1 leek (white part only)
1 branch celery
1 clove garlic
1 sprig each thyme, rosemary, parsley
150 ml ($\frac{1}{4}$ pint) dry white wine
400 ml ($\frac{3}{4}$ pint) *bouillon*
100 g (4 oz) green olives (optional)
40 g ($1\frac{1}{2}$ oz) butter
3 egg whites
oil for deep frying

Drain the anchovy fillets and leave covered until required.

Sift 100 g (4 oz) flour into a bowl, mix in 1 tablespoon olive oil, add a pinch of salt and pour in 150 ml ($\frac{1}{4}$ pint) tepid water. Beat with a hand whisk until smooth then add 3 tablespoons tepid water. Beat again and set aside.

Squeeze and strain the juice of 1 lemon and pour into a soup-plate. Wash and dry the white fish fillets and turn them in the lemon juice to coat on both sides. Leave in the plate until required.

Prick the tomatoes in several places, plunge them into boiling water for 1 minute and then into cold. Skin, cut into halves, remove the seeds with a teaspoon and chop the flesh roughly. Peel and/or trim the onion, carrot, leek and celery and chop finely together. Heat the rest of the olive oil in a shallow saucepan over low heat and add the vegetables, salt and pepper. Leave to cook slowly for 10 minutes, stirring occasionally. Sprinkle with 1 tablespoon flour and, stirring constantly, colour to the golden stage. Add the peeled clove of garlic, chopped tomato flesh, herbs tied together, wine, *bouillon*, salt and pepper and cook over low heat for 20 minutes.

Meanwhile throw the olives into a pan of boiling water and boil for 3 minutes. Drain and set aside. Pat the anchovy fillets with kitchen paper until dry and pound them with the butter to a smooth paste.

Beat the egg whites to a stiff peak. Fold them into the reserved batter; do not stir or beat. Heat the oil for frying, dry the fish, dip into the batter and fry for 6 to 7 minutes. Arrange on a heated serving dish and keep hot.

Remove the herbs from the sauce, add the olives and beat in the anchovy butter with a hand whisk. Pour into a heated sauceboat.

Garnish the fish with slices of lemon and serve immediately with the sauce handed separately.

The farmers who raise *pré-salé* lamb in the meadows bordering the coast of Brittany and Vendée take home vast quantities of mussels, when in season. Here they grow on chestnut posts sunk into the sandy beach so that each in-coming tide submerges them. With this treatment they grow plump and tender and fit to be served with the regional sauce which is a treat in itself. Accompanied by many slices of country bread and many bottles of the local white wine called *gros-plant* this is a memorable meal for a party.

Mouclade bretonne
(Mussels in White Wine Sauce)
Serves 6

3.5 litres (6 pints) mussels
3 medium-large onions
1 large clove garlic
75 g (3 oz) butter
salt, black pepper, cayenne, saffron
2 tablespoons brandy
400 ml ($\frac{3}{4}$ pint) dry white wine
1 teaspoon flour
4 tablespoons double cream

Scrape and wash the mussels thoroughly in several changes of water and remove the beard. Discard any that are open. Place in a large pan with no other ingredients and set aside.

Peel the onions and garlic. Chop the onions medium-fine. Heat half the butter in a large shallow pan over medium heat and when foaming add the onions and a little salt. Stir well, reduce the heat and cook slowly until the juices are rendered and reabsorbed. Stir with a wooden spoon and when the onions start to colour add the garlic. Mix well and add the brandy and white wine, heat for a moment and ignite. When the flames die down add a generous pinch of cayenne, the same amount of saffron and plenty of pepper. Remove from the heat but keep the pan in a warm place.

Soften the remaining butter in a bowl.

Place the pan of mussels over a fairly high heat, cover, and in about 5 minutes they will have opened. Reserving the liquor, remove a half-shell from each mussel and put those on the other half-shell into a large well-heated dish. Cover and keep hot over a pan of simmering water.

Strain the mussel liquor through a sieve lined with tissues into the sauce and place the pan over a high heat for about 5 minutes to reduce the contents. Meanwhile mix the flour into the softened butter with a fork and beat in the cream. As soon as the sauce has reduced by half remove the pan from the heat, beat in the cream and butter mixture until smooth and bring the sauce back to the first bubbles of boiling point over reduced heat. Strain through a sieve over the mussels and serve immediately.

The delectable concoction of mussels, garlic and parsley known in the dialect of La Rochelle as *les moucles persillées* is served either as a main course or first course.

Moucles persillées
(Mussels with Garlic Crumbs)
Serves 2 as a main course,
4 as a first course

1.2 litres (2 pints) mussels
75 g (3 oz) slice stale white or rye bread
1 clove garlic
50 g (2 oz) butter
2 tablespoons chopped parsley
salt, black pepper

Scrape and wash the mussels thoroughly in several changes of water and remove the beard. Discard any that are open. Place in a large pan over a fairly high heat, cover and in about 5 minutes they will have opened. Remove a half-shell from each one and set aside the mussel on the other half-shell. Discard the liquor.

Rub the bread into fine crumbs and set aside. Peel and chop the garlic. Melt the butter in a *sauteuse* or very large frying pan over medium heat and when foaming add the garlic and parsley and cook until the garlic is blond in colour.

Add the breadcrumbs, stir well and, if required, add a little more butter. The mixture should be soft when served. Put the mussels in their half-shell into the pan and mix well with the garlic, parsley and breadcrumbs. Season with a little salt and plenty of pepper. Reduce the heat to low, cover and cook gently for a few moments to mix the ingredients and make the mussels soft. Serve immediately.

One of the simplest country methods of cooking white fish fillets presents them with a ready-made sauce and with their flavour well preserved.

Filets de poisson au citron
(Fillets of Fish with Lemon)
Serves 4

1 large, thin-skinned lemon
4 large fillets of white fish
50 g (2 oz) butter
salt, black pepper

Heat the grill to maximum.

Squeeze the lemon and strain the juice. A large, thin-skinned lemon should give about 4 tablespoonsful.

Wash the fish quickly under cold running water and dry thoroughly. Grease a large *gratin* dish thickly with some of the butter, sprinkle with salt and pepper and place the fillets in it, head to tail. Pour the lemon juice over them, season again and dot with the rest of the butter cut into little pieces. Place the fish under the grill, not too close to the element, and cook for 10 to 15 minutes, basting three or four times. The length of cooking time will depend on the thickness of the fish. Test by piercing the fillets with a sharp-pointed knife.

Serve immediately in the same dish.

The French country recipe for cooking large fish, either whole or in big pieces, is very suitable for the extra large herring and mackerel we find in certain seasons in our own markets. Grey mullet too, or any firm-fleshed fish, is delicious cooked with vegetables in this old-fashioned way.

Poisson en daube
(Braised Fish with Herbs)
Serves 4–6

1 large fish (about 1–1.5 kg [2–3 lb])
225 g (8 oz) each carrots, leeks (white part only), onions
25 g (1 oz) each chives, parsley
100 g (4 oz) sorrel (optional)
salt, black pepper
2 tablespoons olive or corn oil
peel of 2 small oranges
1 small sprig each thyme, rosemary
1 bay leaf
150 ml (¼ pint) dry white wine
4 tablespoons brandy or dry vermouth

Clean the fish and remove the scales by scraping from tail to head with a knife blade. Cut off the fins and tail. If it is to be cooked whole, do not remove the head. Otherwise remove the head and cut the fish into 225 g (8 oz) pieces. Wash under cold running water and dry well. Peel and/or trim the carrots, leeks and onions, and chop them finely with the chives and parsley, and sorrel if used. Season well.

Pour the oil into a large heavy iron *cocotte*, spread half the vegetables over it, place the fish on top, season well and cover with the remaining vegetables and the orange peel cut into pieces. Add the thyme, rosemary and bay leaf tied together, then add the wine and brandy or vermouth. Cover with a tightly fitting lid and cook over minimum heat until the fish is tender when pierced with a skewer (about 1 hour depending on the thickness of the fish). If the pan lid does not fit tightly place a piece of greaseproof paper over the rim of the pan and force the lid down over it. If an earthenware casserole is used, bake in the oven at 170°C, 325°F, Gas 3 for about 1½ hours.

To serve, remove the herbs and orange peel, arrange the fish in a heated dish and pour the vegetables and juices around it.

French gastronomers have, of recent years, banded together against the traditional complication of their classic dishes, preferring and furthering the progress of 'La Nouvelle Cuisine'. This new form of cooking uses first quality ingredients in the simplest way, to produce delicious results. In many cases the dishes resemble old country recipes like the one given below. *Sauce aux câpres* comes from Normandy where the cream produced on the farms is as thick and rich as our own Devonshire and Jersey creams.

Raie aux câpres
(Skate with Caper Sauce)
Serves 4

4 pieces skate (about 225 g [8 oz] each)
1 large onion
1 litre (1¾ pints) water
3 tablespoons tarragon-flavoured wine vinegar
1 sprig each thyme, rosemary, marjoram
salt, black pepper
sauce aux câpres (see following recipe)

Brush the fish well under cold running water with a small hand brush. Peel and quarter the onion. Put the water in a large pan and add the fish, vinegar, onion, herbs tied together, salt and pepper and place over low heat. Bring very slowly to boiling point, then poach gently for 10 to 15 minutes depending on the thickness of the fish. Watch it carefully because skate cooks quickly, and can easily fall apart. When tender, drain and place the fish on a heated serving dish. Cover and keep hot while making the *sauce aux câpres*. Pour the sauce over the fish and serve immediately.

Sauce aux câpres
(Caper Sauce)

2 tablespoons capers
3 tablespoons tarragon-flavoured wine vinegar
150 ml (¼ pint) thick double cream
salt, black pepper

Drain the capers and set them aside.

Pour the vinegar into a small stainless steel or lined saucepan and boil it down rapidly over a high temperature until ½ teaspoon remains. Draw the pan from the heat, stir in the cream with a wooden spoon, season with salt and pepper and when liquid replace the pan over moderate heat. Bring to boiling point and, stirring constantly, boil for 2 minutes. Add the capers and when boiling again cook for 1 more minute only.

Filets de sole aux champignons
(Fillets of Sole in Mushroom Sauce)
Serves 4

4 fillets of sole or other white fish
175 g (6 oz) mushrooms
juice 1 lemon
2 shallots
60 g (2½ oz) butter
salt, black pepper
2 tablespoons water
150 ml (¼ pint) dry white wine
2 teaspoons flour
150 ml (¼ pint) milk

Heat the oven to 190°C, 375°F, Gas 5.

Wash the fish quickly under cold running water and dry thoroughly. Peel, trim and slice the mushrooms and turn them immediately in half the lemon juice to prevent discolouration. Peel and finely chop the shallots. Thickly grease a shallow earthenware dish with 15 g (½ oz) butter and sprinkle with salt, pepper and the chopped shallots. Fold over the fillets into half their lengths and place them in the dish side by side, alternating them so that the fold of one lies next to the open ends of the one beside it. Mix the water with the wine and pour over the fish. Season lightly and cover with well-buttered foil. Bake for 15 minutes or until tender when pierced with a knife point.

Meanwhile melt half the remaining butter in a saucepan over moderate heat and when foaming add the mushrooms and salt, mix well, cover and cook until the juice is rendered and reabsorbed. Remove from pan and set aside. Wipe the pan clean. Melt the remaining butter and when foaming work in the flour with a wooden spoon. Remove from the heat.

When the fish is cooked remove the fillets to a heated serving dish (reserving the wine), cover and keep hot in the oven, heat turned off and door slightly open. Strain the wine into the flour and butter mixture and add the shallots to the mushrooms. Beat the sauce until smooth, return to the heat and cook for 5 minutes, stirring constantly, until reduced a little. Remove the pan from the heat and beat in the milk. When smooth add the mushrooms and shallots and cook for a further 5 minutes until thick. Test for seasoning and correct if necessary, add lemon juice to taste and pour the sauce boiling hot over the fish. Serve immediately.

Gratin de sole à la Gironde
(Baked Sole with Fresh Herbs)
Serves 6

25 g (1 oz) butter
15 g (½ oz) flour
6 fillets of sole or brill
salt, black pepper
2 shallots
175 g (6 oz) mushrooms
50 g (2 oz) gruyère cheese
2 tablespoons chopped parsley
1 tablespoon chopped chives
5 tablespoons stale white breadcrumbs
150 ml (¼ pint) dry white wine
150 ml (¼ pint) chicken *bouillon*

Heat the oven to 180° C, 350° F, Gas 4.

Butter a large *gratin* dish, or other shallow ovenproof dish, with half the butter. Sprinkle thickly with flour, shake out the excess and set aside until required. Wash the fish quickly under cold running water and dry thoroughly. Season with salt and pepper.

Peel and chop the shallots and mushrooms, grate the cheese. Mix the shallots and mushrooms with the parsley and chives and set aside. Melt the remaining butter in a frying pan and when foaming, fry 3 tablespoons breadcrumbs until pale gold in colour. Drain on absorbent paper until required.

Sprinkle the remaining breadcrumbs in the prepared dish and cover with half the herb mixture. Season well and cover with the seasoned fish, placing the fillets head to tail. Scatter with the rest of the herb mixture. Season lightly. Mix the wine with the *bouillon* and pour down the sides of the dish. Toss the buttered crumbs and grated cheese together and sprinkle over the contents to cover.

Bake for 25 to 35 minutes until the *gratin* is browned and crusted and the liquid bubbling.

Serve immediately with small new potatoes.

Filets de sole au vin blanc
(Fillets of Sole in White Wine)
Serves 4

4 fillets of sole or other white fish
2 shallots
40 g (1½ oz) butter
salt, black pepper
2 tablespoons water
150 ml (¼ pint) dry white wine
3 tablespoons *chapelure* (see page 67)
juice ½ lemon

Heat the oven to 180°C, 350°F, Gas 4.

Wash the fish quickly under cold running water and dry thoroughly. Peel and finely chop the shallots. Thickly butter a shallow earthenware dish with 15 g (½ oz) butter and sprinkle with salt, pepper and the chopped shallots. Fold over the fillets into half their lengths and place them in the dish side by side, alternating them so that the fold of one lies next to the open ends of the one beside it. Mix the water with the wine and pour it over the fish. Sprinkle with salt and pepper, dot with the remainder of the butter cut into very small pieces and scatter the *chapelure* over to cover completely. Balance a piece of foil lightly over the fish and bake for 10 minutes, remove the foil, baste with the juices and bake for a further 10 minutes until browned and crusted.

Sprinkle with lemon juice to taste and serve immediately.

Pain de thon
(Tuna Mould)
Serves 6

450 g (1 lb) fillets of whiting
1 lemon
1 sprig each thyme and rosemary, or 1 branch fennel
salt, black pepper
300 g (10 oz) canned tuna
2 tablespoons stale breadcrumbs
4 tablespoons olive oil
½ teaspoon paprika
3 large eggs
2 tablespoons chopped parsley
2 tablespoons chopped chives
2 tablespoons chopped chervil (optional)
herb mayonnaise (see page 71)
2 teaspoons concentrated tomato purée

Wash the whiting fillets quickly under cold running water and dry thoroughly. Cut off the peel and pith of the lemon with a sharp knife, down to the pulp, and cut the lemon into thin slices. Place the whiting fillets in one layer in a large pan, cover barely with water and add the lemon slices, reserving 2 for flavouring. Add the thyme and rosemary or fennel, salt and pepper, and bring slowly to boiling point over low heat. Allow to simmer for 5 minutes, then drain and set aside.

Drain the tuna fish and pat with kitchen paper to absorb any excess oil. Shred finely with a fork. Shred the cooked fish and mix the two. Add the breadcrumbs, oil, salt and pepper, and the paprika. Mix well and pass the mixture through a *mouli-légumes* or vegetable mill. Test for seasoning, correct if necessary, and add the lemon juice from the reserved slices to sharpen the flavour. Heat the oven to 190°C, 375°F, Gas 5.

Break the eggs into a mixing bowl and beat with a fork, mix in the chopped herbs and beat again before adding to the fish mixture. Line a cake tin with well-buttered foil and pour in the mixture. Place in a baking tin half-filled with hot water and bake for 50 minutes. When firm in the centre remove from the oven and leave until cold. Refrigerate overnight.

One hour before serving make the mayonnaise as advised, and beat in the concentrated tomato purée *gradually* after the vinegar is added. Proceed as indicated, transfer to a sauceboat and chill until required.

Unmould the fish on to a serving dish, garnish with parsley sprigs and serve with the mayonnaise handed separately.

Truites à la bretonne
(Trout with Shrimps and Potatoes)
Serves 4

4 trout (about 225 g [8 oz] each)
450 g (1 lb) potatoes
2 tablespoons capers
5 tablespoons corn oil
seasoned flour
50 g (2 oz) butter
175 g (6 oz) peeled shrimps
salt, black pepper
2 tablespoons chopped parsley

Clean and gut the trout and scrape away the dark membrane inside. Remove the tail and fins. Wash quickly under cold running water and wrap in a clean kitchen towel until required.

Peel and wash the potatoes, cut into large dice and dry thoroughly. Drain the capers. Heat 3 tablespoons oil in a *sauteuse* or large iron frying pan over medium heat and when hot add the potatoes, colour to the golden stage on all sides and leave to cook until tender inside and crisp outside. Drain the potatoes and pour away the oil.

Meanwhile dip the trout in seasoned flour and shake to remove any excess. Heat a serving dish in a slow oven. Heat the remaining oil in another pan and cook the trout for about 15–20 minutes, turning them over when one side is coloured golden brown.

Drain the trout, arrange in the serving dish, cover, and keep hot.

Wipe out the potato pan with kitchen paper, replace the pan over moderately high heat and melt the butter until foaming. Add the potatoes, capers and shrimps, season and mix well. Shake the pan constantly to prevent sticking and when piping hot pour this mixture around the trout. Sprinkle with chopped parsley and serve very hot.

The trout farms of the Dordogne have a recipe for marinating their fish which allows it to be kept for several weeks and thus tide over less plentiful times. The same recipe can be used for medium sized herring or small mackerel.

Truites marinées
(Marinated Trout)
Serves 8

8 trout or herring or small mackerel (about 175 g [6 oz] each)
8 teaspoons coarse sea salt
32 cloves
32 black peppercorns
1 large carrot
1 medium sized onion
600 ml (1 pint) dry white wine
150 ml (¼ pint) tarragon-flavoured wine vinegar
2 bay leaves
4 sprigs parsley
salt, black pepper

recipe continues overleaf

Clean and gut the trout and scrape away the dark membrane inside. Remove the scales (if any) by scraping from tail to head with knife blade. Remove the head, fins and tail, wash well and dry thoroughly. Spread the inside of each fish with 1 teaspoon sea salt, 4 cloves and 4 peppercorns and place the fish in a shallow ovenproof dish.

Peel the carrot and onion and slice thinly, put them in a pan with the wine, vinegar, bay leaves, parsley, salt and pepper. Bring slowly to boiling point and simmer for 15 minutes. Heat the oven to 180°C, 350°F, Gas 4.

Pour the marinade over the fish and simmer gently in the oven for 30 minutes. Leave until cold, cover with foil and refrigerate.

To serve, drain the number of fish required, remove the skin and separate into fillets. Arrange on a serving dish, garnish with sprigs of parsley and slices of lemon. Serve with the following sauce handed separately.

Sauce au citron
(Lemon and Herb Sauce)

$\frac{1}{2}$ teaspoon salt
2 teaspoons lemon juice
6 tablespoons olive oil
3 tablespoons chopped parsley
3 tablespoons chopped chervil or tarragon

Dissolve the salt in the lemon juice, then beat in the oil until the mixture is thick and cloudy. Mix in the chopped herbs and test for seasoning, adding a little more lemon juice if necessary.

Truites à la normande
(Trout with Cider and Mushrooms)
Serves 4

4 trout (about 225 g [8 oz] each)
2 shallots
225 g (8 oz) button mushrooms
juice 1 lemon
60 g (2½ oz) butter
salt, black pepper
5 tablespoons strong dry cider
3 tablespoons double cream

Clean and gut the trout and scrape away the dark membrane inside. Remove the tail and fins. Wash quickly under cold running water and wrap in a clean kitchen towel until required.

Heat the oven to 200°C, 400°F, Gas 6.

Peel and chop the shallots finely. Wipe the mushrooms with a damp cloth, trim the stalk end, slice thinly and sprinkle with lemon juice to prevent discolouration.

Butter a shallow ovenproof dish with 15 g ($\frac{1}{2}$ oz) butter, place the vegetables in one layer covering the bottom, arrange the trout on top, season well and dot with remaining butter. Cover with foil and bake for 15–20 minutes or until tender when pierced with a pointed knife.

When the trout is cooked, transfer to a heated serving dish, remove the top skin, cover with foil and keep hot in the oven, heat turned off and door slightly open.

Pour the cider into the cooking dish and mix well with a wooden spoon. Empty the contents into a small saucepan, place over moderate heat and reduce by half. Draw the pan from the heat, add a tablespoon of the juices to the cream, pour this mixture into the pan, stir well, reheat without boiling and pour over the fish. Serve immediately.

The rivers of Alsace produce magnificent trout and those weighing 450 g (1 lb) are considered average. The following recipe for cooking trout in Riesling, the wine best suited to their delicate flavour, can also be used for salmon trout. The quantities given can be doubled or trebled according to the weight of the fish but the cooking time should be increased by no more than 10 minutes for each 450 g (1 lb).

Truite au Riesling
(Trout Baked in Riesling)
Serves 2

1 trout or piece of salmon trout (about 450 g [1 lb]
1 medium sized onion
1 medium sized carrot
60 g (2½ oz) butter
salt, black pepper
1 bay leaf
1 sprig dried thyme
1 sprig parsley
2 tablespoons water
150 ml (¼ pint) Riesling or other dry white wine
juice ½ lemon

Heat the oven to 200°C, 400°F, Gas 6.

Clean and gut the trout and scrape away the dark membrane inside. Remove the tail and fins. Wash quickly under cold running water and wrap in a clean kitchen towel until required.

Peel the onion and carrot and chop medium-fine. Melt a third of the butter in a saucepan over moderate heat and when foaming add the vegetables, mix well and add salt. Reduce the heat to low, cover the pan as tightly as possible and cook the vegetables very slowly for 15 minutes without colouring. The tightly closed pan and the salt will make them render their juices. When the onions are soft and the carrots cooked, pour this mixture into a shallow *gratin* dish, season with pepper, add herbs and place the fish on top. Mix the water with the wine and pour it over the fish. Cover with a piece of buttered foil and bake for 15 minutes. Turn the fish and cook for a further 15 minutes. When cooked, the fish should be easily pierced with a pointed knife. Transfer the fish to a heated serving dish, remove the top skin, cover with foil and keep hot in the oven, heat turned off and door slightly open. Strain the wine and juices into a saucepan, add lemon juice to taste, place over high heat and reduce by half. Remove the pan from the heat and, with a hand whisk, beat in the remainder of the butter, cut into small pieces, until the sauce is cloudy and slightly thickened. Garnish the fish with parsley and serve the sauce separately in a small heated sauceboat.

Chapter Seven

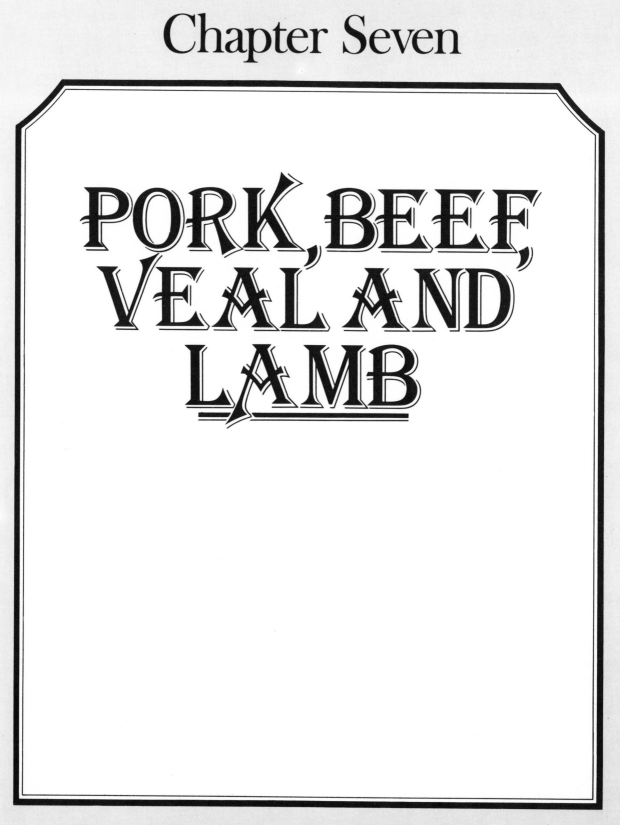

PORK, BEEF, VEAL AND LAMB

Pork

Pork is perhaps the most popular meat in French country households and has been since the days of ancient Gaul. Then the forests that covered the land produced an abundant fodder of acorns, and pigs abounded. The Roman conquerors approved and improved this husbandry, as much for feeding the Gauls as for providing Rome and eventually many other parts of Italy with pork fat and similar delicacies. To overcome the problems caused by slow transport they introduced their method of pickling with salt, and pork proved to be the perfect meat for this process.

And so the pig population increased and prospered through the centuries. In fact, in the 12th century there were few bourgeois inhabitants of Paris who did not own two or three piglets that roamed the streets feeding on refuse. They flourished in this way until the reign of Louis le Gros when disgrace struck their kind. One of the King's sons riding down a narrow thoroughfare of the city was thrown from his horse when a piglet ran between his horse's legs. The King's son died next day and raising pigs in the streets of Paris was banned by royal decree.

Banished to the country, pigs have continued to provide the best meat at the lowest cost ever since. That fact, and the ancient method of preserving still used in farmhouses all over the country, could account for the diversity of pork recipes that exist in the French repertory of meat dishes.

Certain basic pork ingredients are essential in French cooking, notably the pickled belly of pork cooked in the piece in many excellent, economical country dishes, and also used as *lardons*, the short strips that flavour vegetable dishes, meat casseroles and omelettes.

Pickled pork can be bought at all butchers' shops in this country, but the farmer's wife in France prepares it herself, very simply, in order to have a constant supply. Her method makes it much more savoury, economical and convenient to store than that bought in the butchers' shops.

Petit salé
(Pickled Pork, dry-curing method)

1.5 kg (3 lb) fat belly of pork
3 teaspoons saltpetre (obtainable at
   chemists' shops)
salt, black pepper

Cut the pork into 3 oblong pieces, and remove the rind from the one reserved for *lardons*. Do this by placing the pork flat on the board, rind side down, and with a very sharp knife press down on the rind while cutting and rolling back the meat at the same time. Reserve the rind for *paupiettes de boeuf* (see page 99). Jab the 3 pieces of pork all over on both sides with a pointed knife, piercing right through. Sprinkle each side in turn evenly with ½ teaspoon saltpetre, rub it in with the palm of the hand, sprinkle with salt, rub this in, and then sprinkle again with salt and coarsely ground black pepper, making sure that the entire surface and sides are treated. Place in an earthenware dish and cover with a plastic colander. Leave in a cool airy larder.

Turn the meat after 3 days. Turn again after another 3 days and if the surface is dry, sprinkle with a little more salt. Leave for a
recipe continues overleaf

further 3 days. Brush off excess salt, wipe with a clean dry cloth, wrap in waxed paper or foil and refrigerate. The piece reserved for *lardons* should be rolled tightly before wrapping.

Prior to cooking, pickled pork must be well washed under cold running water and then blanched, i.e. placed in a pan of boiling water, boiled for 5 minutes, drained and dried, and then used as directed.

For use as *lardons*, one or two slices 1 cm ($\frac{1}{2}$ inch) thick should be cut into strips the size of the little finger, blanched and used as directed, but do not add salt in the preparation of the dish. Add it after testing, during the cooking.

To store a larger quantity of pickled pork, scald an earthenware crock with boiling water, dry thoroughly and rub with salt, place the pieces of prepared pork in it, layering them with a sprinkling of coarse sea salt, a sprig of thyme, a bay leaf, a few black peppercorns and a few cloves in between each layer. Cover the crock with cheesecloth and store in a cool airy place.

Beekenofe alsacien
(Alsace Hotpot)
Serves 4

225 g (8 oz) onions
225 g (8 oz) young carrots
1 kg (2 lb) potatoes
350 g (12 oz) boned blade of pork
225 g (8 oz) shoulder of lamb
225 g (8 oz) shoulder of veal
salt, black pepper
about 400 ml ($\frac{3}{4}$ pint) Riesling or other dry
    white wine
25 g (1 oz) butter

Heat the oven to 180°C, 350°F, Gas 4.

Peel and slice the onions and carrots finely and the potatoes thickly. Remove the rind from the pork, trim the other meats and cut them all into 5 cm (2 inch) pieces. Butter a large ovenproof dish and spread half the potatoes over the bottom, season lightly and cover with half the onions and then half the carrots. Place the three kinds of meat on top, season lightly and cover with the remaining onions and carrots and a final layer of potato slices. The potato slices should be placed in overlapping rows to cover the rest completely. Pour enough wine down the side of the dish to barely cover the ingredients. Sprinkle with a little salt and pepper, dot with flecks of butter, cover with a buttered paper and the lid and bake for 2 hours in the centre of the oven. Remove the paper and allow the top layer of potatoes to brown and crisp.

Serve immediately in the cooking dish.

Lean pork chops can often be a little dry when cooked, but the farmhouse method eliminates this disappointment and produces a succulent dish for entertaining.

Côtes de porc poivrade
(Pork Chops in Piquant Sauce)
Serves 6

6 thick pork chops
about 10 black peppercorns
3 medium sized onions
1 carrot
2 sprigs thyme
1 bay leaf
salt, black pepper
5 tablespoons dry white wine
5 tablespoons red or white wine vinegar
1 shallot
40 g (1½ oz) pork dripping
1 teaspoon potato flour or cornflour
5 tablespoons double cream

Prepare the meat overnight. Trim the chops neatly and arrange in one layer in a shallow earthenware dish. Crush the peppercorns. Peel and slice 2 onions and the carrot finely and spread out over the meat with the thyme, bay leaf, salt and crushed peppercorns. Mix the wine and vinegar and pour down the sides of the dish, cover and leave in a cool place until required. Do not refrigerate. Turn the meat over next morning and rearrange the vegetables on top. Peel and chop the remaining onion and the shallot medium-fine.

Drain and dry the meat, reserving the marinade. Melt the dripping in a *sauteuse* or large frying pan over medium heat and colour the chops golden brown on both sides. Reduce the heat to low, cover and cook slowly until tender.

Remove to a heated serving dish, cover and keep hot. Pour away excess fat from the pan and in the remainder colour the chopped onion and shallot golden brown. Strain the marinade over them, season well, increase the heat to reduce the liquid by half, scraping the bottom of the pan with the back of a fork to release the meat residue. Strain and return the sauce to the pan over low heat.

Mix the potato flour or cornflour into the cream until smooth, stir into the pan and simmer until thick. Do not boil fast. Pour the sauce over the pork chops and serve immediately with *riz au vin* (see page 56).

If the dish has to wait before being served, cover with foil and keep hot in a warm oven.

The following delicious pork dish is a great favourite for family reunions because it can be prepared beforehand and then takes a short time to cook and serve.

Croquettes de porc
(Pork Croquettes)
Serves 4

150 ml ($\frac{1}{4}$ pint) milk
75 g (3 oz) stale breadcrumbs
2 medium sized eggs
12 small potatoes
12 small onions (pickling size)
450 g (1 lb) sparerib of pork
3 large shallots
40 g ($1\frac{1}{2}$ oz) butter
salt, black pepper, nutmeg
250 ml (8 fl oz) dry white wine
1 tablespoon olive or corn oil
seasoned flour
1 clove garlic
1 sprig each thyme, rosemary
1 bay leaf
150 ml ($\frac{1}{4}$ pint) *bouillon*
2 tablespoons boiling water
1 tablespoon chopped parsley

Pour the milk over the breadcrumbs and set aside. Separate the eggs. Peel the potatoes and onions.

Remove the rind and bone from the pork, cut the meat into pieces and pass them through the coarse grid of the mincer. Peel and finely chop the shallots. Melt a third of the butter in a frying pan over low heat and, when foaming, add the shallots and cook until soft without colouring. Stir frequently. Meanwhile squeeze all moisture from the breadcrumbs and when the shallots are cooked, put the crumbs into a large bowl, add the shallots and pan juices and mix well. Add the minced pork, salt, pepper and grated nutmeg and mix very thoroughly. Stir in 5 tablespoons of the wine and, when incorporated, add the egg yolks one at a time, stirring the mixture well before adding the next one. Test for seasoning, correct if necessary and set aside.

Put the remaining butter and the oil into a *sauteuse* or very large frying pan over low heat and colour the onions well on one side.

Meanwhile beat the egg whites to a very stiff peak and fold them into the meat mixture a third at a time. Do not stir or beat.

Turn the onions over, take up a well-heaped tablespoon of pork mixture, carefully roll it in seasoned flour and place immediately in the pan as each one is rolled. Arrange in one layer and colour to golden brown on all sides, shaking the pan frequently to prevent sticking. When well crusted, add the peeled garlic, and herbs tied together. Mix the *bouillon* and remaining wine, pour down the sides of the pan and reduce the heat to low. Bring slowly to boiling point and place the potatoes here and there among the onions and the croquettes. Season lightly with salt and pepper, cover, and cook for 30 minutes until the potatoes are tender, shaking the pan occasionally.

To serve, remove the herbs, carefully transfer the croquettes to a heated serving dish with a slotted spoon, arrange the onions and potatoes around them, and keep hot in the oven. Pour the boiling water into the pan, scrape up the meat residue from the bottom with the back of a fork, stir well and pour boiling hot over the meat and vegetables. Sprinkle with chopped parsley and serve immediately.

For 6 to 8 people double the quantities given and cook either in two pans or in a heavy roasting tin, covered with foil and as in a *sauteuse* on top of the cooker.

Saucisses de porc (see page 93).

No part of the pig is wasted when it is slaughtered on the farm. Even the head is used to provide a number of excellent and very economical meals.

Fromage de tête de porc
(Farmhouse Brawn)
Serves 8–10

1 fresh pig's head
4 shallots
4 carrots
4 onions
1 large leek
1 clove garlic
1 sprig each parsley, marjoram, thyme
1 bay leaf
1 tablespoon salt
10 black peppercorns
4 cloves
black pepper (optional)
2 tablespoons finely chopped parsley

Have the butcher split the head into halves and remove the ears. Place cut side down in a sieve and pour fast-boiling water over the skin. Drain and scrape off any blemishes. Peel and finely chop the shallots. Peel the carrots and onions and trim the leek, cut them all into pieces. Place the pig's head, carrots, onions, leek and peeled garlic in a large pan, cover generously with cold water and bring slowly to boiling point over low heat. Skim off the froth that rises and when clear add the herbs tied together, seasoning and cloves. Cover and cook, simmering steadily, for 2 hours or until the meat detaches itself from the bones. Remove the meat, skin and fat from the bones, cut into pieces and place in a large bowl. Add the brains, and the tongue skinned and cut into small pieces. Mash with a fork and mix well. Test for seasoning, add black

Boeuf batellerie (see page 95).

pepper if necessary so that the mixture is well flavoured. Mix in the chopped shallot and parsley, and stir to incorporate thoroughly. Pour into 2 wetted moulds and when cold refrigerate until required.

To serve, cut into slices and arrange on a large serving dish surrounded by lettuce leaves. Hand French mustard separately and a mixed green salad tossed in *vinaigrette* dressing (see page 61).

Being made of fresh meat this brawn should be eaten within a week.

The French market gardener pulls his new crop of turnips when they are very small and tender, in fact not much bigger than golf balls. His wife cooks them with pork to make a very savoury country dish.

Either fillet or loin of pork, boned and rolled, is suitable for this dish. Ask the butcher to remove the rind from the pork before boning and rolling it. The fillet may require a little extra barding fat to cover the top and sides before it is rolled and tied. Loin is less dry and its own fat is sufficient for cooking.

Filet de porc aux navets
(Fillet of Pork with Turnips)
Serves 6

about 20 small fresh turnips
1 tablespoon pork dripping
1.5 kg (3 lb) boned and rolled fillet end of
    leg or loin of pork
salt, white and black pepper
2 tablespoons boiling water
2 teaspoons castor sugar
5 tablespoons *bouillon*
1 tablespoon concentrated tomato purée
2 tablespoons hot water

recipe continues overleaf

Peel the turnips. Melt the pork dripping in a heavy metal *cocotte* and when hot, brown the meat well on all sides. As it renders its fat pour off the fat into a *sauteuse* or large frying pan until there is the equivalent of 2 tablespoons left in the *cocotte*. Season the meat lightly with salt and white pepper, add the boiling water, cover and reduce the heat to low. Cook slowly for about 1½ hours.

Reheat the pork fat in the *sauteuse* over medium heat, arrange the whole turnips in one layer, sprinkle with sugar and colour well on all sides. Reduce the heat and cook until tender, shaking the pan occasionally to turn them over. Season with salt and black pepper. Heat the oven to 150°C, 300°F, Gas 2.

Remove the meat from the *cocotte* when tender, carve into thick slices, arrange on a heated serving dish with the turnips, cover tightly with foil and keep hot in the oven. Mix the *bouillon* with the tomato purée. Pour off excess fat from the *cocotte*, place it back over low heat, add the hot water and deglaze the pan by scraping the meat juices from the bottom with the back of a fork. Allow to bubble, then add the *bouillon* mixture. When bubbling fast pour over the turnips and meat. Cover again and leave for 10 minutes in the oven before serving, to allow the flavours to be absorbed.

Pork marinated and cooked in red wine with glazed onions is a popular dish in French farmhouses for special occasions.

Filet de porc en venaison
(Marinated Pork with Onions)
Serves 6

1 large carrot
1 medium sized onion
1 clove garlic
8 black peppercorns

1.5 kg (3 lb) boned and rolled fillet end of leg or loin of pork
6–8 pork bones, chopped
1 sprig each thyme, parsley
1 bay leaf
300 ml (½ pint) red wine
5 tablespoons red or white wine vinegar
salt
2 tablespoons pork dripping
6 tablespoons *bouillon*
1 tablespoon concentrated tomato purée
12 small onions (pickling size)
25 g (1 oz) butter
2 teaspoons cornflour
1 tablespoon water

See introduction to previous recipe for instructions on preparing the meat.

Peel the carrot, onion and garlic. Dice the carrot and onion. Crush the peppercorns. Place the meat in an earthenware dish just big enough to hold it with the bones, carrot and onion, garlic, and herbs tied together. Mix the wine and vinegar and pour over the meat. Sprinkle lightly with salt and scatter the crushed peppercorns on top. Cover and leave in a cool place for 24 hours but do not refrigerate. Turn the meat over 4 times during this period.

When ready to cook drain the meat and vegetables thoroughly, reserving the marinade. Melt the dripping in a large iron *cocotte* over medium heat, dry the meat thoroughly and brown well on all sides. Set aside and then brown the vegetables and bones until well coloured. Return the meat to the pan.

Mix the *bouillon* with the tomato purée, add to the marinade and pour over the meat, bones and vegetables. Reduce the heat to very low and when simmering point is reached cover and continue simmering slowly for about 1½ hours or until tender. Do not remove the lid except to turn the meat 2 or 3 times. Meanwhile peel the small onions, melt the butter in a large frying pan and when foaming half-cook the onions, browning them on both sides. Remove with a slotted spoon and place around the meat after turning it for the last time.

When the meat is cooked the marinade should have reduced by about a quarter. If not, tilt the lid to half-cover the pan and simmer a little faster to reduce.

Remove the meat from the pan and place on a heated serving dish, place the onions in another dish, cover both with foil and keep hot in a warm oven. Strain the marinade and return it to the pan, discarding the chopped vegetables and bones. Mix the cornflour with the water and stir until smooth, add a little marinade and mix well before returning it to the pan. Beat until incorporated and leave to simmer for 5 minutes. Correct the seasoning if necessary.

To serve, carve the slices of pork required for the first serving, pour a little of the sauce over them and the rest into a heated sauceboat. Arrange the onions on either side of the meat and serve immediately.

Crackling on pork is the Englishman's prerogative. Ignored by the Americans, unknown to the Belgians, it is a revelation to the French, who, in return, have a way of cooking pork for a family gathering which makes the everyday roast into a party piece with a very subtle flavour.

Palette de porc en croûte
(Blade of Pork Baked in Pastry)
Serves 6–8

2 kg (4 lb) blade of pork
400 g (14 oz) frozen puff pastry
3 long branches tarragon
salt, white and black pepper
100 g (4 oz) jar strong French mustard
1 egg yolk
1 tablespoon water

Ask the butcher to bone the joint and remove the rind which should be reserved for use in *paupiettes de boeuf* (see page 99).

Remove the pastry from the freezer 1½ hours before required and leave at room temperature. Heat the oven to 230 °C, 450 °F, Gas 8.

Wash the tarragon under running water and shake dry. Remove the leaves from the stalk and set aside.

Make frequent holes in the meat with a skewer and push half the tarragon leaves into them. Season lightly with salt and both peppers, form neatly but do not tie, and brush thickly all over with mustard.

Roll out the pastry into a large rectangle and spread out the remaining tarragon leaves in the centre. Place the meat on top and fold over the pastry to make a neat package, moistening the edges to seal. Make a small hole in the centre of the pastry. Cut a strip of foil 5 cm (2 inches) wide, wind it round a pencil to make a small funnel and insert it in the hole. Beat the egg yolk with the water and use to glaze the pastry. Place in the oven. After 20 to 30 minutes when the crust has coloured to the golden brown stage reduce the heat to 200°C, 400°F, Gas 6, cover with a piece of buttered greaseproof paper and continue cooking for a further 1½ hours.

To serve, place the *palette en croûte* on a heated serving dish and carve at the table.

Ragoût de porc
(Ragoût of Pork with Tomatoes)
Serves 6

3 medium-large onions
1.5 kg (3 lb) thick end of belly of pork
  (with rib bones)
1 tablespoon flour
600 g (1¼ lb) large tomatoes (preferably
  Mediterranean variety)
1 sprig each thyme, rosemary
1 bay leaf
salt, white and black pepper
6–8 medium sized potatoes

Peel and halve the onions and set aside.

Remove the rind from the pork, cut the thick meaty end into serving portions and divide the bones and their meat into 6 pieces.

Put the latter into a *sauteuse* or large frying pan over low heat to render their fat. When coloured to golden brown remove with a slotted spoon, drain on absorbent paper and place in a *cocotte* or heavy iron pan. In the fat in the *sauteuse* colour the rest of the meat to golden brown, drain and add to the *cocotte*. Sprinkle with flour and stir to coat the ingredients. Add the whole tomatoes, the onions, the herbs tied together and seasoning. Add enough warm water to barely cover the ingredients. Increase the heat to medium and when boiling reduce to low, cover and simmer for 1½ hours.

Peel the potatoes and after the time indicated place them on the surface of the *ragoût*, cover and simmer for 30 minutes. When the potatoes are tender remove the herbs and serve immediately.

This *ragoût* is excellent when reheated, but remove any left-over potatoes, before refrigerating in a closed container, if it is to be served a second time.

The harsh climate of the Auvergne produces hard workers with large appetites. In consequence, farm cooks in that region are known for their hearty savoury dishes.

Petit salé auvergnat aux lentilles vertes
(Pickled Pork with Green Lentils)
Serves 4

12 small onions (pickling size)
450 g (1 lb) small green lentils (obtainable at
  health food shops)
1 kg (2 lb) pickled belly of pork (see page 83)
1 tablespoon pork dripping
salt, black pepper
3 cloves garlic
1 sprig each thyme, rosemary, marjoram
1 bay leaf
1 branch celery
25 g (1 oz) butter
2 tablespoons chopped parsley

Peel the onions and set aside. Wash the lentils in cold water, drain, and leave to soak in more cold water until required. Place the pork in a large pan and cover generously with cold water. Place over very low heat, bring slowly to boiling point and boil for 5 minutes. Drain the meat, wash well under cold running water and dry thoroughly.

In a large *cocotte* or heavy iron pan melt the pork dripping and when hot place the meat in the pan, add the onions, sprinkle well with pepper but do not salt. Turn these ingredients over from time to time until they are well coloured.

Crush the garlic slightly but do not peel, and add to the pan with the herbs and celery tied together. Drain the lentils and spread them over the meat and onions. Cover generously with boiling water, bring back to boiling point, cover and simmer over very low heat for 2 hours.

To serve, remove the pork with a slotted

spoon and increase the heat under the pan to absorb any excess liquid. Carve the meat into thick slices and keep hot between two soup-plates over a panful of boiling water. Cut the butter into small pieces and mix well into the lentils, correct the seasoning if necessary and stir in the chopped parsley. Pour into a heated serving dish and arrange the pork on top in overlapping rows. Serve immediately.

Any pork not required at the meal should be left whole and pressed between two plates with a weight on top. When cold and thinly sliced it is served with eggs instead of bacon, or with a green salad as a snack. An extra piece is often cooked for this purpose.

———————————————

Like most simple dishes, home-made sausages can be perfection if the right proportions are respected. This excellent old recipe belonged to a farmer who made his sausages in the autumn to last through the winter. Some of the meat was eaten fresh, and some was put into skins and hung in festoons over the open fireplace, absorbing the wood smoke that rose from it.

Saucisses de porc
(Home-made Sausages)
Serves 6

1.2 kg (2½ lb) sparerib of pork
225 g (8 oz) pork fat (flair or back fat)
   (obtainable at supermarkets)
2 teaspoons salt
½ teaspoon each white pepper, black pepper,
   cinnamon, allspice, nutmeg
100 g (4 oz) finely chopped shallot or onion
2 tablespoons finely chopped parsley
2 large egg yolks
flour
1 teaspoon pork dripping

Remove rind and bones from the pork and fat and pull off the thin membrane from the flair if used. Cut lean and fat into cubes and pass them alternately through the coarse grid of the mincer. Spread the meat on the cutting board, sprinkle with salt and both peppers and the spices. Mix well by folding sides to centre and kneading the seasonings into the meat. Spread out again, scatter with shallot or onion and with parsley and knead again to incorporate thoroughly. Bind with the beaten egg yolks and when well mixed form into a thick roll and divide into 12 portions. Shape into thick sausages or round cakes and flour lightly. If not to be cooked immediately wrap the sausagemeat in foil, without flouring it, and refrigerate.

Place a heavy iron frying pan, dry, over medium heat and leave for a few moments. Add the pork dripping and when melted swirl it round the pan to coat completely, add the sausages or sausage cakes and colour to the golden stage on one side. Reduce the heat and cook slowly for 10 minutes shaking the pan occasionally to prevent sticking. Turn the meat over, increase the heat to brown the second side, reduce the heat and cook slowly for 10 minutes shaking the pan frequently. Drain well on kitchen paper before serving.

This meat is delicious when used in the recipe given overleaf for *saucisses au chou*.

If made in quantity for freezing, do not add the parsley and shallots/onion until ready to cook.

The sausages of Auvergne are famous throughout France and serving them with cabbage cooked in white wine and herbs is a favourite winter dish. The nearest equivalent to these sausages in England are those sold in Italian delicatessen shops, but better still, use home-made sausage cakes (see page 93).

Saucisses au chou
(Sausages with Cabbage)
Serves 4

2 large carrots
2 medium-large onions
1 kg (2 lb) firm hearted green cabbage
salt, white and black pepper
2 tablespoons pork dripping
1 sprig each thyme, rosemary, marjoram
1 bay leaf
1 clove garlic
150 ml ($\frac{1}{4}$ pint) dry white wine
5 tablespoons *bouillon*
4 large sausages or sausage cakes

Peel and slice the carrots and onions thickly and set aside. Remove the coarse outer leaves of the cabbage, cut the heart into 4 sections and remove the hard core, leaving just enough to hold the leaves together. Place in a large pan in one layer and cover with boiling water, add salt, and when boiling again cook for 5 minutes. Drain into a colander and hold under cold running water for a minute. Squeeze the cabbage between the palms to expel all moisture and chop coarsely.

In a *cocotte* or heavy iron pan melt the pork dripping, add the carrots and onions, and the herbs tied together. Sauté over very moderate heat for 10 minutes, stirring frequently to avoid burning the fat, then add the peeled and crushed garlic and the cabbage. Mix well and cook together until the moisture from the cabbage has evaporated, then add the wine and *bouillon* mixed and season with salt and both peppers. Cover and simmer until the cabbage is tender.

Meanwhile, rub a piece of buttered paper over a large frying pan. Prick the skins of the sausages and cook slowly until browned. If sausage cakes are used, brown them first quickly over moderate heat then cook slowly over reduced heat for 10 minutes. Turn them over and repeat to cook the other side, shaking the pan frequently.

When the cabbage is cooked remove the lid from the pan and increase the heat under it to evaporate any remaining liquid. Place the sausages or sausage cakes on top, pour any juices over the cabbage, reduce the heat to low, cover and leave for 10 minutes to mingle the flavours.

To serve, remove the herbs from the pan and arrange sausages or sausage cakes and vegetables in a heated dish. Serve very hot with strong French mustard.

94

Beef

There was a time when the wine harvest of the Rhône valley was transported by barge which plied up and down the River Rhône starting from Valence. Local wine experts deplored the arrival of the railway, being of the opinion that the slow gentle progress of the barges did nothing to upset the wine in transit. Slow and gentle too was the life of the bargees, living and eating aboard as they still do, and cooking their food with the same lack of haste. They produce some particularly succulent dishes by this method.

Boeuf batellerie
(Beef in Red Wine and Anchovy Sauce)
Serves 4

700 g (1½ lb) chuck steak (cut in one large
    slice 2.5 cm [1 inch] thick)
salt, black pepper
1 teaspoon dried thyme
2 cloves garlic
3 tablespoons chopped parsley
2 carrots
2 onions
2 shallots
3 tablespoons red wine vinegar
4 tablespoons olive oil
150 ml (¼ pint) red wine

Sauce
2 shallots
1 clove garlic
2 tablespoons chopped parsley
2 tablespoons chopped onion
1 tablespoon chopped chives
5 anchovy fillets
25 g (1 oz) butter
300 ml (½ pint) red wine

Leave the meat in one whole slice, just nick the rim of skin to prevent it curling. Place on a board and sprinkle with salt, pepper and dried thyme. Crush the garlic but do not peel, chop roughly and mix with the parsley. Strew this mixture over the meat on both sides and press lightly into the surface. Peel and slice the carrots, onion and shallots, and put half of them into a deep earthenware dish just large enough to hold the meat, place the meat on top and cover with the remainder of the vegetables. Beat the vinegar and oil together until thick and cloudy, beat in the wine until incorporated and pour down the sides of the dish. Cover and leave to marinate overnight but do not refrigerate. Turn once during this time. The meat can be marinated for 5 or 6 days if a fuller flavour is preferred.

Transfer the meat to a heavy cast-iron *cocotte*, strain the marinade over it and discard the vegetables. Cover, place over very low heat and bring slowly to boiling point. If cooked in the oven, preheat the oven to 170°C, 325°F, Gas 3. In either case cook as slowly as possible until tender and do not remove the lid except to turn the meat over once. Cooking time should be between 1½ to 2 hours on top of the cooker, a little longer in the oven.

Meanwhile, prepare the ingredients for the sauce. Peel and roughly chop the shallots and garlic. Mix well with the parsley, onion and chives, chop very finely together and set aside. Drain and dry the anchovies, chop finely, mix with the butter and pound on a plate with the back of a wooden spoon until smooth. Roll into a ball and chill until required.

When the meat is tender the liquid in the *cocotte* will have almost evaporated, leaving only the oil. Remove the meat, drain off the oil, wipe out the pan, pour in the wine for the sauce and add the chopped shallot mixture. Stir well, replace the meat, cover and simmer for 15 minutes. Remove the meat to a heated serving dish, cover with foil, tucking it under the dish to seal, and keep hot.

Divide the anchovy butter into small pieces, remove the pan from the heat and beat the butter into the sauce with a whisk. Pour over the meat, cut the meat into 4 portions and serve immediately with jacket potatoes.

Boeuf en boulettes
(Beefballs in Madeira Sauce)
Serves 4

450 g (1 lb) tomatoes
200 g (7 oz) pickled belly of pork (see page 83)
2 medium sized onions
1 tablespoon chopped parsley
450 g (1 lb) frying steak or fillet end of skirt
salt, black pepper
1 large egg
flour for coating
40 g (1½ oz) butter
6 tablespoons Madeira
2 tablespoons cream

Prick the tomatoes in several places, plunge them into boiling water for 1 minute then into cold. Skin, cut into halves, remove the seeds with a teaspoon, and chop the flesh roughly.

Wash the pickled pork in several changes of cold water, cut into *lardons* the size of the little finger, throw into a pan of boiling water and simmer for 5 minutes. Drain and dry thoroughly. Peel and slice the onions and chop very finely with the *lardons* and parsley. Cut the steak into pieces and pass them through the fine grid of the mincer. Spread the mince out on the cutting board in a large circle. Season with pepper and a little salt and spread the pork and onion mixture thinly over it. Knead with the hands bringing sides to centre to blend thoroughly. Bind with beaten egg and form into 8 or 10 balls. Roll on a lightly floured board to coat.

Heat the butter in a *sauteuse* or large frying pan over low heat and when foaming colour the meat balls on all sides. Keep the heat low to avoid burning the butter. When well coloured and firm add the Madeira and chopped tomato flesh, season lightly and, when simmering, cover and cook slowly for 30 minutes until the tomatoes are reduced to purée.

Remove the pan from the heat, stir the cream into the sauce, correct the seasoning and serve immediately with mashed potatoes.

Many classic dishes have suffered through the passing of time. Familiarity has substituted one ingredient for another until finally the fine flavours of the original dish are lost. The French country woman changes her recipes as little as she changes her opinions, and she demands the best of burgundies for preparing her *boeuf bourguignon*. Her husband hands over a bottle of his best quite willingly in anticipation of what then becomes a connoisseur's dish cooked in the old country manner.

Boeuf bourguignon
(Beef in Red Wine and Herb Sauce)
Serves 6

1.2 kg (2½ lb) lean topside of beef
225 g (8 oz) pickled belly of pork (see page 83)
20 small onions (pickling size)
1 tablespoon pork dripping or pure lard
2 tablespoons flour
750 ml (1¼ pints) burgundy or other full-bodied red wine
1 sprig each rosemary, thyme, parsley
1 bay leaf
salt, black pepper, nutmeg

Cut the beef into large cubes. Wash the pickled pork in several changes of cold water, cut into *lardons* the size of the little finger, throw into a pan of boiling water and simmer for 5 minutes. Drain and dry thoroughly. Peel the onions.

Put the *lardons* into a heavy iron *cocotte* over low heat to render their fat, and when it covers the bottom of the pan with a thin film add the onions and cook until *lardons* and onions are well coloured. At this point remove them with a slotted spoon and set aside. Add the pork dripping or lard and when melted over low heat colour the beef on all sides. Sprinkle with flour and brown it lightly, mixing it into the fat with a wooden spoon. Add the wine and beat with a birch whisk until smooth. Add just enough warm water to cover the ingredients, and the herbs tied together. Season well with salt, pepper and a generous grating of nutmeg. Increase the heat a little and bring to boiling point. As the first bubbles break reduce the heat to low, add the *lardons*, cover and leave to simmer for 1½ to 2 hours. Add the onions 20 minutes before the end of this time.

Serve with a dish of floury boiled potatoes or small new potatoes.

The following dish of tender steak in a mustard and cream sauce is ideal for entertaining because it requires little preparation and is cooked in very few minutes.

Eminces de boeuf
(Steak in Mustard and Cream Sauce)
Serves 6

6 medium-thin slices rump steak
4 shallots
60 g (2½ oz) butter
250 ml (8 fl oz) double cream
1 teaspoon strong French mustard
salt, black pepper
1 teaspoon potato flour or cornflour (optional)
1 tablespoon water (optional)

Trim the steak, removing all fat, and cut into 1 cm (½ inch) wide strips. Cut these into 5 cm (2 inch) lengths. Peel and finely chop the shallots. Melt half the butter in a *sauteuse* or large frying pan and when foaming add half the beef and turn the strips over to seal quickly on all sides. They should remain rare inside. Remove from the pan with a slotted spoon and seal the rest in the same way. Add the remainder of the butter and when foaming cook the shallots until melting but not coloured. Stir well, scrape up the meat juices from the bottom of the pan with the back of a fork and add 4 tablespoons cream. Increase the heat and reduce the cream, stirring constantly until it thickens slightly and colours to the blond stage. Stir in the rest of the cream and the mustard. Season well with salt and pepper and stir in the meat and the juices it will have rendered. Bring to the first bubble but do not allow to boil.

If the cream sauce is too liquid, just before adding the meat remove the pan from the heat and stir in the potato flour or cornflour mixed with water. Replace the pan over low heat, bring back to boiling point and allow to bubble for a minute before adding the meat and juices. Do not boil again after adding them.

Serve immediately with *riz au vin* (see page 56) or buttered noodles.

In Provence where the quality of the olives, their oil and the huge locally grown tomatoes is far superior to that of the local red wine, beef is cooked with herbs and these vegetables in a light white wine to produce a fine aromatic dish. It can be made in a large quantity because it reheats perfectly.

Estouffade de boeuf à la niçoise
(Beef in White Wine, Tomato and Herb Sauce)
Serves 6

1 kg (2 lb) chuck steak (cut in one thick slice)
225 g (8 oz) pickled belly of pork (see
  page 83)
2 large onions
2 cloves garlic
1 sprig each rosemary, marjoram, thyme
1 bay leaf
2 cloves
6 large Mediterranean tomatoes or 12 large
  domestic tomatoes
750 ml (1¼ pints) dry white wine
300 ml (½ pint) water
3 tablespoons olive oil
2 tablespoons flour
2 teaspoons coarse sea salt
black pepper
24 small black olives
1 tablespoon chopped parsley

Cut the beef into large cubes. Wash the pickled pork in several changes of cold water, cut into *lardons* the size of the little finger, throw into a pan of boiling water and simmer for 5 minutes. Drain and dry thoroughly. Peel and quarter the onions. Peel and crush the garlic. Tie the herbs together and stick the cloves into the bay leaf. Prick the tomatoes in several places, plunge them into boiling water for 1 minute and then into cold. Skin, cut into halves, remove the seeds with a teaspoon and place upside down to drain. Mix the wine with the water.

Heat the oil in a heavy iron *cocotte* or braising pan over medium heat and colour the *lardons* until golden and crisp. Remove with a slotted spoon and set aside. Colour the onions, remove from the pan and colour the meat on all sides. Remove the meat, sprinkle the flour into the fats and stir until incorporated. Add the garlic, herbs tied together, wine and water. Return the browned ingredients to the pan and bring slowly to boiling point. Remove any froth as it rises and when the surface is clear, season with the salt and plenty of pepper. Reduce the heat to low, cover, and simmer slowly for 1½ hours. Meanwhile roll the olives lightly with the end of a bottle to free the stones, and remove the stones with a pointed knife.

Remove the meat, onions and *lardons* from the pan with a slotted spoon and place them in a clean *cocotte* or braising pan, cover with the drained tomatoes placed cut side down and arrange the stoned olives on top.

Sieve the liquids into a wide-topped bowl and remove excess fat first with a metal cooking spoon then by passing bands of kitchen paper over the surface until it is clear. Pour over the meat, cover and simmer for a further 40 minutes after boiling point is reached. Remove the lid for the last 10 minutes to reduce the sauce.

Pour the *estouffade* into a deep, heated serving dish, sprinkle with chopped parsley and serve with boiled potatoes.

Paupiettes de boeuf
(Stuffed Steak Rolls)
Serves 6

6 large thin slices buttock steak (175 g [6 oz] each)
175 g (6 oz) pickled belly of pork (see page 83)
1 clove garlic
2 tablespoons chopped parsley
½ teaspoon dried thyme
salt, black pepper, mixed spice
1 medium sized onion
1 large carrot
1 large piece pork rind (reserved from other recipes, see pages 83 and 91)
1 sprig thyme
1 bay leaf
150 ml (¼ pint) dry white wine
150 ml (¼ pint) *bouillon*
2 teaspoons potato flour or cornflour
2 tablespoons water

Ask the butcher to flatten the steak with a cleaver. Trim the edges and reserve the trimmings. Wash the pickled pork in several changes of cold water, cut into *lardons* the size of the little finger, throw into a pan of boiling water and simmer for 5 minutes. Drain and dry thoroughly. Chop finely with the peeled garlic and the steak trimmings and mix in the parsley, dried thyme, pepper and mixed spice. Test for seasoning and then add a little salt if necessary. Divide this stuffing into 6 portions, wrap a piece of steak around each one to form a neat roll and tie with string.

Peel and slice the onion, peel and grate the carrot. Place the pork rind, fat side downwards, in a heavy iron *cocotte* and cover with the onion and carrot. Add the sprig of thyme and bay leaf. Place the beef rolls on top, cover and set the *cocotte* over medium heat for 30 minutes. Add the wine, increase the heat until the contents bubble fast, add the *bouillon* and when boiling again cover, reduce the heat and simmer very gently for about 45 minutes.

Meanwhile, heat the oven to 240°C, 475°F, Gas 9. When the meat is easily pierced with a pointed knife, place the *cocotte* in the oven and baste several times until the meat is well coloured on top. This will take about 15 minutes.

To serve, remove the meat with a slotted spoon and place on a heated serving dish. Cover and keep hot. Remove the pork rind from the pan and skim off all fat from the sauce, first with a metal kitchen spoon then with bands of kitchen paper passed over the surface. Bind the liquid with the potato flour or cornflour mixed with water, allow to bubble for a few minutes and pour over the meat. Serve immediately with jacket potatoes.

Veal

The lush pastures of Normandy produce fine cattle, thick cream, apples and calvados. When they are richly combined to celebrate a special occasion they produce a memorable dish.

Côtes de veau normande
(Veal Chops with Apples, Cream and Calvados)
Serves 6

150 g (5 oz) butter
6 thick veal chops with bone (about 200 g [7 oz] each)
salt, black pepper, sugar
300 ml (½ pint) double cream
6 tablespoons calvados (apple brandy)
1 kg (2 lb) dessert apples (Cox's or Golden Delicious)

Heat the oven to 180°C, 350°F, Gas 4.

Melt half the butter in a *sauteuse* or large iron frying pan over medium-low heat and, when foaming, put in the chops and colour to golden brown on both sides. Place them in a shallow ovenproof dish just large enough to hold them in one layer, season well, cover with foil folded tightly under the rim of the dish and place in the oven on the middle shelf.

Deglaze the pan with the cream, scraping the bottom with the back of a fork to release the meat juices, heat slowly until simmering and reduce by a third. Add the calvados, mix well, pour over the meat, cover again and continue cooking for about 30 minutes or until tender.

Wipe out the pan with paper. Peel and core the apples and cut each one into 8. Melt the remaining butter over medium heat and, when foaming, cook the apple slices until golden on both sides. Sprinkle lightly with sugar and glaze on both sides, shaking the pan frequently to prevent sticking. Remove the pan from the heat and cover.

To serve, arrange the chops on a heated serving dish, correct the seasoning of the sauce if necessary, and pour it over the chops. Place the apple slices around the dish and serve very hot with boiled rice or buttered noodles.

Foie de veau au madère
(Calves' Liver with Madeira)
Serves 4

450 g (1 lb) calves' or lambs' liver
2 large shallots
75 g (3 oz) butter
150 ml (¼ pint) Madeira
salt, black pepper

Have the liver cut in large slanting pieces 2 cm (¾ inch) thick. Remove all membrane and cut the liver into strips 4 cm (1½ inches) long. Peel and finely chop the shallots. Cut 25 g (1 oz) butter into small pieces and set aside.

In a *sauteuse* or large frying pan placed over low heat, melt the rest of the butter and when liquid add the liver, stir well to coat with butter and cook very gently until just firm, no more. Remove with a slotted spoon and place on a warm plate over a pan of hot water. Do not cover.

In the butter remaining in the pan cook the shallots without colouring, add the Madeira, bring to boiling point and reduce by a third. Lower the heat, add the liver and the juices it will have rendered, season and sauté for a further 2 minutes. The liver must remain soft and still pink inside. It will continue cooking by its own heat and that of the sauce, so do not overcook in the first place.

Draw the pan away from the heat and beat in the small pieces of butter with a birch whisk until the sauce is cloudy and slightly thickened. Pour into a heated serving dish and serve immediately with boiled rice or buttered noodles.

Making a good dish for visitors out of inexpensive ingredients is a strong point with farming wives, as the following recipe proves.

Ris de veau aux épinards
(Sweetbreads with Spinach in Cream Sauce)
Serves 6

1 kg (2 lb) sweetbreads, fresh or frozen
1.5 kg (3 lb) fresh spinach or 1 kg (2 lb) frozen spinach
300 g (10 oz) sorrel (optional)
1 carrot
1 onion
900 ml (1½ pints) water
1 bay leaf
salt, black pepper, nutmeg
1 tablespoon tarragon-flavoured wine vinegar
2 shallots
60 g (2½ oz) butter
1 tablespoon flour
300 ml (½ pint) double cream
2 medium sized egg yolks

If frozen sweetbreads are used, remove from freezer and place in the refrigerator overnight, then thaw at room temperature.

If fresh spinach is used, wash it in several changes of cold water and remove the centre rib. Wash again but do not dry. Set aside until required. Wash and prepare the sorrel in the same way, if used.

Peel and slice the carrot and onion, place in a large pan over medium heat with the water, bay leaf and a little salt and pepper. Add the vinegar and when boiling reduce the heat and simmer fast until reduced by half. Remove the pan from the heat, add the sweetbreads and sufficient boiling water (if necessary) to barely cover them. Bring slowly to boiling point over low heat and simmer for 20 minutes. Drain in a colander and hold under cold running water for 1 minute. Remove all skin and membrane from the sweetbreads and set aside.

Peel and chop the shallots finely. Melt two thirds of the butter in a *sauteuse* or heavy iron frying pan and when foaming add the shallots and cook over low heat until they start to colour. At this point add the sweetbreads, cut into thick slices if large. Season with salt and pepper, cover and leave to braise slowly for 20 minutes.

Meanwhile, cook the fresh spinach, in just the amount of water clinging to the leaves, in a dry pan over moderate heat for 5 minutes, stirring frequently. By this time the leaves will be wilted and soft. Drain (reserving the liquid) and squeeze dry between the palms. If frozen spinach is used, drop the block into a dry pan and cook only until the iced water has melted. Drain (reserving the liquid) and squeeze dry. Cook the sorrel, if used, in the reserved liquid for 2 minutes only, drain and squeeze dry. Mix the spinach and sorrel, squeeze again and chop roughly. Heat the oven to 200°C, 400°F, Gas 6.

Remove the sweetbreads from the pan with a slotted spoon and in their butter and juices dry out all remaining moisture from the spinach and sorrel. Season well with salt, pepper and a generous pinch of grated nutmeg. Sprinkle evenly with flour, mix well and add half the cream. Mix again and pour this preparation into a large *gratin* dish or other shallow ovenproof dish. Arrange the sweetbreads on top. Beat the egg yolks into the rest of the cream, season with salt and pepper and pour over the contents of the dish. Dot with the remainder of the butter cut into little flecks and place in the oven to heat thoroughly and colour lightly on top without reaching boiling point.

Tendron de veau à la provençale
(Breast of Veal with Tomatoes)
Serves 6

1.5 kg (3 lb) breast of veal
5 large Mediterranean tomatoes or 10 large
    domestic tomatoes
2 medium sized onions
1 large shallot
2 cloves garlic
3 tablespoons olive oil
1 piece dried orange peel
1 sprig each thyme, rosemary, tarragon
1 bay leaf
1 tablespoon concentrated tomato purée
150 ml ($\frac{1}{4}$ pint) dry white wine
salt, black pepper, cayenne

Ask the butcher to cut the veal into 2.5 cm
(1 inch) thick slices. Cut them into serving
pieces about 5 cm (2 inches) long.

Prick the tomatoes in several places, plunge
them into boiling water for 1 minute and then
into cold. Skin, cut into halves, remove the
seeds with a teaspoon, and chop the flesh
roughly. Peel and finely chop the onions and
shallot, and peel and crush the garlic.

Heat the oil in a *sauteuse* or heavy frying pan
over moderate heat and colour the meat to the
blond stage. Remove it from the pan and keep
warm between two plates. Add the onions,
shallot and orange peel to the pan and in
the same oil cook them until the onions are
tender, without colouring. Add the tomato
flesh, the herbs tied together, the garlic, and
tomato purée. Pour in the wine and mix until
smooth, add the meat, salt, pepper and a good
pinch of cayenne. Cover and leave to simmer
over very low heat for about $1\frac{1}{2}$ hours. If the
sauce, which should be thick when cooked,
becomes too thick before the meat is tender,
add a little boiling water but only a tablespoon at a time. Cook until the veal is tender
when pierced with a pointed knife.

Serve with boiled rice.

Lamb

The frugality of the peasants of the
Auvergne is legendary. They find it no
hardship to eat their native chestnuts as a
main course instead of meat. But when on
special occasions they cook a leg of lamb,
it is memorable. The aroma of it while
cooking is almost as good as the meat
itself.

Gigot d'Auvergne en cocotte
(Braised Leg of Lamb with Onions)
Serves 8

8 large flat onions
2 cloves
12 shallots
25 g (1 oz) butter
4 white peppercorns
6 black peppercorns
salt, nutmeg, allspice, ginger
1 sprig thyme
1 bay leaf
2 kg (4 lb) leg of spring lamb
8 medium sized potatoes
150 ml ($\frac{1}{4}$ pint) dry white wine

The flat Dutch onions now imported are the
best for this dish. Peel, and stick the cloves
into one of them. Peel the shallots.

Thickly butter a large iron *cocotte*, a Doufeu
or braising pan with half the butter, spread
the onions out in one layer and add the
shallots, lightly crushed peppercorns, salt and
two generous pinches each grated nutmeg,
ground allspice and ginger. Add the herbs
tied together. Make 3 short deep cuts in the
thickest part of the meat and rub a nut of the
remaining butter into each one. Fold back the
shank and place the meat on top of the vegetables. Cover, and if a Doufeu is used fill
the sunken lid with cold water. Place over
medium heat and when the contents of the

pan start to sing, lower the heat immediately to minimum and cook for 1 hour, turning the meat over once. If the onions show signs of sticking to the pan add a little more butter.

Peel and thickly slice the potatoes, season lightly and add to the cooking pot with the wine. Cover again and cook for 1 hour more or until meat is tender and oozes a pink juice when pierced with a metal skewer.

To serve, carve the meat into small thick slices, down to the bone and across the thickest part of the leg. Arrange the slices on a heated serving dish and place the vegetables around them. Strain the sauce over the top and serve immediately.

Garlic would be a superfluous addition to this dish.

––––––––––––––––––

Le gigot boulangère is one of the simplest of all French country dishes, but it has urban gourmets covering hundreds of miles in pursuit of it. As with all perfect dishes, timing and the quality of the ingredients are of the first importance. The lamb, in order to preserve its full flavour, must be cooked only until the skin is crisp and the meat tender, juicy and *still pink inside*. If overcooked, it is ruined. Allow 20 minutes to each 450 g (1 lb), no more. To preserve all flavours and juices, it is traditionally cooked and served in a shallow earthenware dish. A heavy metal roasting tin will serve the same purpose.

Gigot boulangère
(Baked Leg of Lamb with Potatoes)
Serves 8

1 kg (2 lb) medium sized potatoes
2 cloves garlic
2 kg (4 lb) leg of spring lamb
75 g (3 oz) butter
salt, black pepper
2 tablespoons water
1 large onion
1 bay leaf
2 sprigs thyme

Heat the oven to 200°C, 400°F, Gas 6.

Peel and thinly slice the potatoes and leave wrapped in a wet kitchen towel until required. Peel the garlic.

Wipe the leg of lamb with a cloth wrung out in boiling water. Plunge a pointed knife into the knuckle end and insert 1 clove of garlic. Melt the butter slowly in a small pan. Place the meat in a shallow earthenware dish, pour half the butter over it to cover the surface, sprinkle with salt, add the water to the dish and place in the oven. Cook for exactly 20 minutes, basting twice.

Meanwhile, peel and finely slice the onion and chop the remaining clove of garlic. Mix with the potatoes on a cutting board, season well with salt and pepper. Remove the lamb from the oven, cover and keep hot on the side of the cooker. Spread the potato and onion mixture in the bottom of the baking dish, place the herbs on top, and add just sufficient boiling water to barely reach their level. Place on a protective mat over low heat until boiling point is reached again. Replace the meat on the potatoes. Pour over it the rest of the butter and return the dish to the oven. Cook for a further 40 minutes turning the meat twice.

To serve, remove the meat to a heated carving dish, leaving the potatoes in the oven with the heat turned off. Quickly carve the lamb into thick slices, arrange them on top of the potatoes, pour the carving juices over the whole and serve immediately in the cooking dish.

The specially reared lamb known in France as *pré-salé*, named after the coastal salt-meadows on which it is raised, is one of the great treats of that gastronomically-minded country. When grilled it is served under-done, as all except casseroled lamb is served in France.

Côtes d'agneau à la provençale
(Lamb Chops with Aubergines)
Serves 4

150 ml ($\frac{1}{4}$ pint) olive oil
1 large sprig rosemary
2 aubergines (about 700 g [1$\frac{1}{2}$ lb] in all)
salt, black pepper
1 clove garlic
3 tablespoons chopped parsley
4 double lamb chops (cut double thickness)
2 teaspoons dried thyme
2 large Mediterranean tomatoes or 4 large
   domestic tomatoes

Put the olive oil into a small jug and plunge the branch of rosemary, head down, into it. Leave to macerate for 1 hour.

Peel the aubergines with a very sharp knife and cut into thick slices. Sprinkle with salt on both sides, arrange on a plate in one layer, and place another plate on top with a weight on it. Leave for at least 30 minutes. Drain and wash under cold running water, dry well and cut into cubes. Peel the garlic and chop finely with the parsley.

Remove the outer skin of the lamb chops and nick the surrounding fat with scissors to prevent it curling. Brush on both sides with the sprig of rosemary dipped in oil and sprinkle with thyme. Cut the tomatoes into halves, remove the seeds with a teaspoon, sprinkle with salt, pepper and a few drops of oil and push a little of the garlic and parsley mixture into the cavities, reserving some of it for garnishing.

Heat the grill at medium-high temperature. Heat the remaining oil in a large frying pan and when hot sauté the aubergines over medium heat, turning them occasionally and cooking them slowly until tender and coloured to golden brown. When the aubergines start cooking place the tomatoes under the grill, not too near the element, and cook until soft and browned. When cooked place in a ring around a heated serving dish and keep hot. Increase the heat of the grill and cook the chops for 5 minutes on each side. They should be crisp and brown outside and still pink inside when served. Remove the aubergines from the pan with a slotted spoon and place in the centre of the tomatoes. Sprinkle with the rest of the garlic and parsley mixture.

Arrange the chops on another heated serving dish, pour the juices over them, season with salt and pepper and serve meat and vegetables without delay.

Gigot boulangère (see page 103).

Côtelettes d'agneau au vin blanc
(Lamb Cutlets Baked in White Wine)
Serves 4

1 kg (2 lb) potatoes
1 clove garlic
4 lean lamb cutlets, best end of loin (allow
   2 per person if small)
75 g (3 oz) butter
2 tablespoons boiling water
4 tablespoons coarsely chopped onion
salt, black pepper
300 ml ($\frac{1}{2}$ pint) dry white wine
4 tablespoons cold water
$\frac{1}{2}$ teaspoon dried thyme
1 bay leaf

Peel and thinly slice the potatoes. Leave wrapped in a wet cloth until required. Peel and finely chop the garlic.

Trim the lamb cutlets of skin and any excess fat. Melt half the butter in a *sauteuse* or large frying pan over medium heat and when foaming quickly colour the meat to the golden stage on both sides without cooking it. Remove with a slotted spoon and keep hot between two plates. Deglaze the pan with the boiling water, scraping up the meat juices from the bottom with the back of a fork. Pour this over the meat.

Put the rest of the butter in the *sauteuse* over low heat and when foaming add the chopped onion and cook until transparent without colouring. Spread the onion in a large shallow ovenproof dish and place the cutlets on top, season well with salt and pepper, and pour their juices over them. Mix the wine with the cold water and pour half down the sides of the dish, sprinkle with thyme, the crumbled bay leaf and garlic. Heat the oven to 190°C, 375°F, Gas 5. Throw the potato slices into a pan of boiling salted water, and as soon as the water boils again drain them into a colander. Arrange the slices in overlapping rows on top of the meat and pour over them the rest of the wine and water which should just reach their level, no more.

Place the dish in the oven, covered with buttered foil, and bake until the potatoes are tender, basting them once or twice. Remove the foil and increase the heat to 220°C, 425°F, Gas 7, and leave until the potatoes are crusted and brown.

Serve in the same dish.

Tendron de veau à la provençale (see page 102).

Ragoût d'agneau
(Ragoût of Lamb with Potatoes and Herbs)
Serves 4–6

700 g (1½ lb) lean shoulder of lamb
700 g (1½ lb) neck of lamb
1 teaspoon salt
½ teaspoon black pepper
1¼ teaspoons sugar
1 tablespoon pure lard
2 tablespoons flour
4 tablespoons concentrated tomato purée
1 litre (1¾ pints) water
1 sprig each thyme, rosemary, marjoram
1 bay leaf
20 small onions (pickling size)
20 small new potatoes
15 g (½ oz) butter
1 tablespoon chopped parsley

Cut the shoulder meat into 75 g (3 oz) pieces and put them on the chopping board with the neck end chopped at the joints. Sprinkle with the salt, pepper and ¼ teaspoon sugar. Mix well and leave to impregnate for 10 minutes. Melt the lard in a large iron *cocotte* or iron frying pan and colour the meat to the golden stage over moderately low heat to prevent the fat burning. If it turns too dark empty the pan, wipe it out and start again.

Pour off the excess fat, sprinkle the meat with flour and stir it around the pan to coat and allow to colour slightly. Dissolve the tomato purée in the water and pour it over the meat, scraping up the meat juices on the bottom of the pan with the back of a fork and stirring them into the sauce. Add the herbs tied together. Cover and leave to simmer over low heat for 1¼ hours. (Transfer to the oven in a casserole if prepared in a frying pan. Cook at 170°C, 325°F, Gas 3 for 1 hour 30 minutes.)

Meanwhile, peel the onions, scrape the potatoes and leave the latter wrapped in a wet cloth until required.

Melt the butter in a large frying pan and, when foaming, sauté the onions, shaking the pan to coat them on all sides. Sprinkle with the remaining sugar and allow them to glaze and caramelise to the golden stage. Remove the herbs from the sauce, add the onions and potatoes, cover and cook gently for a further 30 minutes.

To serve, remove excess fat from the surface of the liquid first with a metal cooking spoon and then by passing a few bands of kitchen paper over the surface. Sprinkle with parsley and serve immediately.

This dish reheats well if any is left over. Reheat in the oven at 180°C, 350°F, Gas 4, for 35 to 40 minutes with fresh potatoes previously par-boiled for 5 minutes.

Chapter Eight

POULTRY AND GAME

Poultry

The raising of geese in France has always been an important farming activity: the large goose bred mainly around Toulouse, the Gers area, the Landes, and in Strasbourg, for the quality and size of its liver; the smaller one, which after fattening attains a weight of 4.5 kg (10 lb), for the excellence of its flesh when roasted. Not that the large goose provides nothing but its liver for *foie gras:* the rest of this enormous bird is usually made into *confit d'oie.* That delicious and extremely rich form of conserve has been made since culinary records have been kept, to preserve the meat from one season to another. The exquisite flavour of the young goose is brought to perfection when the bird is cooked with chestnuts in the following manner.

L'oie aux marrons
(Goose with Chestnuts)
Serves 12

700 g (1½ lb) chestnuts
1 heart of celery (with leaves)
300 ml (½ pint) chicken *bouillon*
1 young goose (about 4.5 kg [10 lb]),
    including liver
salt, black pepper, allspice
175 g (6 oz) duck and/or chicken livers
350 g (12 oz) chipolata sausages
2 large onions
2 large turnips
2 large carrots
1 small head of celery
1 bay leaf
25 g (1 oz) butter
750 ml (1¼ pints) dry white wine

Slit the chestnuts on the rounded side and place under a preheated medium grill about 10 cm (4 inches) below the element. When the outer skin cracks, peel off both skins, keeping the nuts as whole as possible. Chop the celery heart finely and add to the *bouillon.* Cook the chestnuts in the *bouillon* over a very low heat, uncovered, until tender and the liquid is absorbed. Set aside until required.

Wipe the goose inside and out with a cloth wrung out in boiling water. Pull away any fat clinging to the interior and render it down slowly in a large frying pan. Season the bird inside with salt, pepper and a generous pinch of allspice. Trim the goose liver and extra livers of membrane and slice off any parts stained yellow. Place the livers in the rendered fat and sauté them lightly over low heat until just firm but still soft and pink inside. Remove with a slotted spoon and set aside. Prick the chipolatas and cook them slowly in the same fat until just firm enough to skin. Remove from the pan, skin and cut into 1 cm (½ inch) long pieces. Cut the livers into small cubes about the same size and mix with the chestnuts and chipolatas. Season well, mix again and stuff the interior of the goose with this preparation. Close the aperture by folding the skin over and securing it with trussing pins or wooden cocktail sticks. Tie down the legs and wings to the body by passing a piece of thin string around them and then under the back from one side to the other leaving the breast unrestricted.

Heat the oven to 200 °C, 400 °F, Gas 6. Peel and slice the onions, turnips and carrots medium-thick. Trim the head of celery and cut into short lengths. Mix the vegetables, season well, add the crumbled bay leaf and mix again.

Butter a large flat baking tin or oven dish and spread the vegetables evenly over the bottom. Put the goose on top, melt the butter and pour slowly over the surface. Place the baking tin over very low heat on top of the cooker and colour the underside of the vegetables to the blond stage. This will take about 15 minutes. Pour half the wine around the bird and place in the centre of the oven.

Roast for 45 minutes, basting twice with the pan juices. When the wine has evaporated add the remainder. Reduce the heat to 190°C, 375°F, Gas 5 and continue cooking for a further 1½ hours or until the thickest part of the thigh is tender when pierced with a sharp-pronged cooking fork. If during this time the skin browns too quickly, balance a piece of foil lightly on top of the bird, taking care to remove it to crisp the skin again 10 minutes before taking the goose out of the oven.

To serve, place the goose on a heated serving dish and keep hot in the oven with the heat turned off and the door slightly open.

Strain the contents of the baking tin into a wide bowl, leave the vegetables in a colander to drain, and reserve them (see page 145). Remove the excess fat from the cooking liquor first with a metal cooking spoon and then by passing bands of kitchen paper over the surface until it is clear. Reheat to boiling point in a clean pan and pour into a heated sauceboat.

This noble dish is usually served with a slightly chilled Musigny or if the season has been particularly prosperous it is honoured with a Châteauneuf-du-pape.

The meadows of the Bresse region are thickly speckled with fat white hens and capons, each one a peer of its realm. These hand-raised birds are famous throughout France for the delicacy of their flesh and these are some of the recipes used for cooking them in the farmhouse kitchens of Burgundy.

Poularde à la Carnot
(Stuffed Capon with Spring Vegetables)
Serves 6–8

1 free-range capon (2 kg [4 lb])
100 g (4 oz) mushrooms
2 large shallots
8 small onions
6 small new potatoes
1 clove garlic
6 small spring carrots
4 chicken livers
50 g (2 oz) butter
75 g (3 oz) sausagemeat (see page 93)
salt, black pepper, mixed spice
1 tablespoon chopped parsley
2 medium sized egg yolks
6 tomatoes
1 sprig each thyme, rosemary, parsley
1 bay leaf
3 dessert apples (Cox's or Golden Delicious)
juice 1 lemon
6–8 chipolata sausages
150 ml (¼ pint) dry white wine

Wipe the capon inside and out with a cloth wrung out in boiling water. Peel and trim the mushrooms and slice thickly. Peel and chop the shallots. Peel the onions, potatoes and garlic. Scrape the carrots. Trim the livers, removing any membrane and all parts stained yellow. Melt half the butter in a *sauteuse* or frying pan and when foaming add the shallots and cook over gentle heat for a few minutes,
recipe continues overleaf

111

add the livers and heat for just long enough to make them firm on both sides. They must not cook. Remove them from the pan with a slotted spoon and set the shallots and their juice aside. Chop the livers and mushrooms together finely, mix in the sausagemeat, add the shallots and their juice, season well with salt, pepper and a generous pinch of mixed spice. Mix in the chopped parsley and bind with the beaten egg yolks.

Heat the oven to 190°C, 375°F, Gas 5.

Stuff the bird with three quarters of the stuffing inside and the remainder in the breast cavity. Fold the skin underneath and tuck it under the wings. Butter a large earthenware casserole, put in the capon and arrange the onions, potatoes and carrots around it. Prick the tomatoes in several places, plunge them into boiling water for 1 minute and then into cold. Skin, cut into halves, remove the pips with a teaspoon and place them, cut side down, over the other vegetables. Add the garlic, the herbs tied together, and season well with salt and pepper. Melt the rest of the butter and pour it over the breast of the chicken. Cover and cook in the oven for $1\frac{1}{4}$ hours.

Meanwhile, peel and core the apples, cut each one into 8 and turn in lemon juice to prevent discolouration. Prick the chipolatas and place them round the chicken on top of the other ingredients. Cover and cook for 20 minutes. Add the apples and cook for a further 10 minutes.

To serve, place the chicken on a heated serving dish with the vegetables, chipolatas and slices of apple around it. Cover with foil and keep hot in the oven with the door slightly open.

Remove the herbs from the casserole, add the wine, scrape up the meat residue in the bottom with the back of a fork, mix well and pour into a small saucepan. Test for seasoning and correct if necessary. Place over medium heat, bring to boiling point and allow to bubble for a few minutes. Pour into a heated sauceboat and serve with the chicken immediately.

The in-born sense of economy for which farming people are noted is thrown to the winds during the preparations for a wedding feast. This chicken dish, very popular in Anjou, is cooked with the best of white wine and brandy to produce a particularly delicious sauce.

Poulet Bertrand
(Chicken in Cream and Brandy Sauce)
Serves 6

1 roasting chicken (2 kg [4lb])
40 g ($1\frac{1}{2}$ oz) salted butter
40 g ($1\frac{1}{2}$ oz) unsalted butter
salt, black pepper
150 ml ($\frac{1}{4}$ pint) dry white wine
3 tablespoons brandy
2 large egg yolks
300 ml ($\frac{1}{2}$ pint) double cream

Cut the chicken into serving pieces and wipe with a damp cloth wrung out in boiling water. Pull off any excess fat and render it down over gentle heat in a *sauteuse* or very large frying pan. Add the salted butter and when it foams place the pieces of chicken flat in the pan and brown on both sides. When well coloured put the chicken to drain on kitchen paper. Pour away the fats, wipe out the pan and melt the unsalted butter until foaming. Replace the chicken pieces in the pan so that they do not overlap. Season well with salt and pepper and, shaking the pan constantly, sauté the chicken over increased heat for 2 or 3 minutes. Pour the wine into the pan and bring to boiling point, add the brandy, draw the pan from the heat and ignite the liquids, basting the meat until the flames die down. Cover closely, reduce the heat to low and simmer for 1 hour or until the chicken is tender.

To serve, remove the chicken pieces from the pan with a slotted spoon and arrange in a heated serving dish. Cover and keep hot. Beat the egg yolks into the cream and season lightly. Scrape the bottom of the pan with the sides of a fork to release the meat residue and incorporate it into the sauce. Bring to boiling point and draw the pan from the heat, pour a little of the liquid into the cream, mix well with a wooden spoon and pour this mixture back into the pan stirring constantly until the sauce thickens. The pan can be placed over minimum heat during this operation but on no account must the sauce reach boiling point. Pour the sauce over the chicken and serve immediately with boiled rice.

The country woman's simple method of cooking the Sunday chicken in a big pot with rice, plenty of vegetables and herbs is the recipe that was perfected by Escoffier, although I doubt whether his humble followers are aware of the fact. It is however his attention to detail that makes this homely dish so excellent.

Poulet au riz à la ménagère
(Chicken with Rice)
Serves 8

1 chicken (2 kg [4 lb])
salt, black pepper
200 ml (7 fl oz) cold water
225 g (8 oz) small carrots
4 small onions
2 cloves
1.5 litres (2½ pints) hot water
15 g (½ oz) coarse sea salt
2 large sprigs parsley
1 sprig thyme
1 bay leaf

1 heart of celery
100 g (4 oz) rice
50 g (2 oz) butter

Wipe the chicken inside and out with a cloth wrung out in boiling water. Lightly season the inside with fine salt and a little pepper. Place the bird in a large iron *cocotte* or soup-pan and pour the cold water over it. Cover and place over medium heat. Leave for about 10 minutes until the water has evaporated completely. Meanwhile peel and finely slice the carrots. Peel the onions and stick cloves into 2 of them.

Add the hot water to the pan, then the sea salt, and the herbs and celery heart tied together. Bring very slowly to boiling point and skim off the froth that rises until the surface is clear.

When the pot is boiling steadily, add the carrots, onions and some pepper and reduce the heat to produce a slow simmer. Cover and cook for 1 hour 10 minutes. Meanwhile wash the rice in a fine sieve under cold running water and leave to drain.

After 1 hour 10 minutes, sprinkle the rice around the chicken, increase the heat slightly and when boiling point has been re-established, cover and cook for a further 20 minutes.

Remove the chicken carefully from the pan with 2 slotted spoons and place in a heated serving dish. Cover and keep hot. Remove the herbs from the pan and the cloves from the onions. Stir in the butter cut into small pieces, season well with pepper and pour the vegetables and liquid around the chicken.

Serve at once, very hot, with a bottle of chilled Vouvray.

Poulet à la Montrachet
(Chicken and Mushrooms in Cream Sauce)
Serves 6

1 free-range chicken (2 kg [4 lb])
225 g (8 oz) small spring carrots
225 g (8 oz) small onions (pickling size)
225 g (8 oz) button mushrooms
25 g (1 oz) butter
1 long branch tarragon or 1 sprig each thyme, rosemary, parsley
1 bay leaf
salt, black pepper
150 ml ($\frac{1}{4}$ pint) white burgundy
2 large egg yolks
300 ml ($\frac{1}{2}$ pint) double cream

Wipe the chicken inside and out with a cloth wrung out in boiling water. Cut into 10 serving pieces: 2 drumsticks, 2 thighs, 2 wings and 2 breasts halved. Scrape the carrots and peel the onions. Wipe the mushrooms with a damp cloth and trim the stalks. Melt the butter in a heavy iron *cocotte* over low heat and when foaming add the pieces of chicken, the carrots and onions, and the herbs tied together. Season with salt and pepper, add the wine, cover and cook for 30 minutes, moving the ingredients around occasionally to prevent colouring. When the carrots and onions are tender remove them with a slotted spoon, cover and keep hot over a pan of boiling water.

Slice the mushrooms finely, add to the pan, sprinkle with salt, cover and simmer for a further 20 minutes. Beat the egg yolks into the cream and set aside.

Remove the chicken from the pan to a heated serving dish, place the vegetables around it in small groups, cover with foil and keep hot.

Using the back of a fork, work the meat residue from the bottom of the pan into the cooking juices. Bring to boiling point, remove the herbs, and draw the pan from the heat. Add a tablespoon of pan juices to the cream, stir well and return this mixture to the pan, stirring constantly until thick. Pour immediately over the chicken and serve without delay.

The excellent sauce of this dish is best appreciated when accompanied by plain noodles or boiled rice.

The regional recipes of France have evolved throughout time to complement the local wines. Hence the rich recipes of Burgundy. Poitou and Vendée produce wines of lesser glory and their recipes, in consequence, are more homely—but none the less appetising when served with the 'little' wines of the region.

Fricassée de poulet à la poitevine
(Chicken in Onion Sauce)
Serves 6

1 kg (2 lb) onions
1 chicken (1.5–2 kg [3–4 lb])
salt, black pepper
25 g (1 oz) butter
2 tablespoons flour
2 tablespoons wine vinegar (preferably shallot-flavoured [see page 16])

Peel the onions, quarter them and slice thickly.

Wipe the chicken inside and out with a cloth wrung out in boiling water. Cut into 10 serving pieces: 2 drumsticks, 2 thighs, 2 wings and 2 breasts halved. Season each piece on both sides. Melt the butter in a *sauteuse* or large frying pan over low heat and when foaming add the chicken and colour to the golden stage on both sides. Remove from the pan with a slotted spoon, cover and keep hot. Add the onions to the fats in the pan, season, increase the heat to medium, mix well and colour to the golden stage, moving them around with a wooden spatula to prevent sticking and colouring too fast.

Sprinkle with half the flour and mix in thoroughly before adding the remainder. Cook for a few moments, stirring constantly, reduce the heat to low, add the vinegar, stir well and arrange the chicken on top. Cover and cook slowly for about 40 minutes until the chicken is tender and the moisture from the onions has made the sauce. During this time shake the pan frequently and do not lift the lid except to stir the ingredients twice. Correct the seasoning if necessary and serve very hot with plain boiled potatoes.

Petits poussins au citron
(Spring Chickens with Lemon)
Serves 4

2 *poussins* (450 g [1 lb] each)
1 clove garlic
2 large lemons
2 tablespoons olive oil
2 tablespoons soy sauce
black pepper

Cut the birds into halves down the breastbone and then into quarters. Remove the skin and wing tips and reserve them for *bouillon* (see page 22). Poach the livers in salted water for a few moments, drain and set aside. They must not be cooked hard.

Peel the garlic and crush with the blade of a knife. Peel the lemons thickly, taking care not to include any white pith. Cut the peel into fine strips and then into very small dice. Squeeze the juice from the lemons but do not strain. Beat half the lemon juice into the olive oil, add the soy sauce, diced peel and crushed garlic, season with pepper and beat this marinade well. Pour it into a shallow fireproof dish and place the pieces of chicken in it flesh-side down, pressing the peel into the meat. Leave for at least 2 hours to marinate (overnight if possible), basting occasionally.

Heat the grill to maximum temperature. Place the chicken, in its marinade and still flesh-side down, under the grill about 13 cm (5 inches) from the element and cook for 10 minutes. Turn the pieces over, sprinkle with the rest of the lemon juice and baste with the marinade, pressing the peel into the surface. Reduce the heat slightly and grill for a further 10 minutes until the meat is tender, crisp and well browned. Remove to a heated serving dish and keep hot.

Crush the livers into the pan juices with a fork, beat well, pour over the chicken and serve immediately.

If cooked to serve cold as a picnic dish, leave the chicken to cool in the marinade flesh-side down with the lemon peel pressed into it. When cold drain on absorbent paper, then pack in greaseproof paper and serve with small hearts of lettuce. Salt is not required with this dish. Lemon juice takes its place.

Pintades à l'ancienne
(Old-fashioned Casserole of
Guinea-hen)
Serves 6

2 guinea-hens (about 1 kg [2 lb] each)
salt, black pepper
2 medium sized carrots
1 medium sized turnip
12 small onions (pickling size)
225 g (8 oz) button mushrooms
225 g (8 oz) streaky bacon (in one piece)
1 tablespoon flour
4 tablespoons water
150 ml ($\frac{1}{4}$ pint) dry white wine
2 tablespoons double cream
juice $\frac{1}{2}$ lemon

Cut each of the guinea-hens into 4 pieces.
Sprinkle with salt and pepper and set aside.
Peel and dice the carrots and turnip. Peel the
onions. Wipe the mushrooms with a damp
cloth and trim the stalks. Remove the rind
from the bacon and cut the meat into *lardons*
the size of the little finger. Put them into a
heavy iron *cocotte* over low heat and leave to
render their fat, stirring occasionally. When
coloured to the blond stage, add the diced
carrots and turnip and the whole onions and
colour to the blond stage too. Remove from
the pan with a slotted spoon and set aside.
Put the pieces of guinea-hen into the pan,
turn them over in the fat and, as soon as they
start to colour, sprinkle with flour. Cook for
a few minutes, moving the pieces around with
a wooden spatula occasionally to prevent
sticking. Mix the water with the wine, pour
into the *cocotte*, add the previously cooked
carrots, turnip and onions, and the mushrooms cut into quarters. Cover and leave to
simmer very gently for about 1$\frac{1}{4}$ hours until
tender.

To serve, draw the pan from the heat, stir a
tablespoon of the juices into the cream, pour
this mixture back into the pan and stir well.
Correct the seasoning, if necessary, and add
lemon juice to taste.

Arrange the pieces of guinea-hen in the
middle of a heated serving dish in a mound,
with the vegetables placed around them, and
pour the sauce over the top. Serve with small
new potatoes.

Game

The shooting season brings game in plenty
to the farmhouse table, with hare and
rabbit the most frequent contributions.
Young hare is usually roasted whole and
the mature hare cooked *en civet*, a method
for which the blood of the animal is
essential.

Civet de lièvre
(Jugged Hare)
Serves 6

1 large hare (2–2.5 kg [4–5 lb])
1 tablespoon wine vinegar
225 g (8 oz) pickled belly of pork (see page
   83)
20 small onions (pickling size)
2 cloves garlic
40 g (1$\frac{1}{2}$ oz) butter
3 sugar lumps
salt, black pepper
2 tablespoons flour
4 tablespoons brandy
600 ml (1 pint) red wine
300 ml ($\frac{1}{2}$ pint) water
3 sprigs thyme
1 sprig rosemary
1 bay leaf

Have the hare skinned, paunched and cut into
serving pieces. Reserve the blood and put it
into a small bowl with the liver. Add the
vinegar, cover and set aside. Wipe the hare

with a cloth wrung out in cold water and dry thoroughly. Wash the pickled pork in several changes of cold water, cut into *lardons* the size of the little finger, throw into a pan of boiling water and simmer for 5 minutes. Drain and dry thoroughly. Peel the onions. Peel and crush the garlic.

Melt the butter in a *cocotte* or heavy iron pan over low heat, add the *lardons* and when they start to render their fat, add the onions and sugar and colour the *lardons* and onions to golden brown. Remove with a slotted spoon and set aside. Add the pieces of hare, season lightly, increase the heat slightly and colour well on both sides. Sprinkle with flour and allow it to colour lightly, moving the meat around meanwhile with a wooden spatula to prevent sticking. Remove the pan from the heat, pour in the brandy, ignite, shake the pan, baste the meat, and when the flames die down add the wine and water. Return the pan to the heat and bring to boiling point. Reduce the heat to low, add the crushed cloves of garlic and the herbs tied together. Cover and simmer very slowly for about $1\frac{1}{2}$ hours or until the hare is almost cooked.

Add the *lardons* and the small onions and continue cooking until the hare is tender. Transfer the meat and onions to another heavy pan, strain the cooking liquid over them and simmer over very low heat for 20 minutes uncovered.

To serve, chop the liver finely, cut the butter into little flecks and mix them both into the blood. Draw the slowly-simmering pan from the heat, gradually add this binding, stirring constantly, correct the seasoning, transfer meat, onions and sauce to a heated serving dish and serve immediately with jacket potatoes or *marrons braisés* (see page 135).

If no *cocotte* is available, this dish can be prepared in a large frying pan, transferred to an earthenware casserole and cooked in the oven at 170° C, 325° F, Gas 3.

The bold Duke of Burgundy, nicknamed Jean-sans-peur, earned this title by gaining possession of Paris for a brief spell in the 15th century; this city then represented the government of France. The Duke soon paid for this fine prize with his life, but his name has lived on in the splendid dish that is still served by the old farming families of Burgundy.

Râble de lièvre Jean-sans-peur
(Roast Saddle of Hare with Grapes in Brandy)
Serves 6

50 g (2 oz) fresh pork fat
1 young hare (1.5–2 kg [3–4 lb])
4 shallots
1 clove garlic
2 carrots
2 onions
10 black peppercorns
1 sprig each thyme, rosemary
750 ml ($1\frac{1}{4}$ pints) dry white burgundy
225 g (8 oz) large green seedless grapes
2 tablespoons brandy
100 g (4 oz) streaky bacon
salt, black pepper
2 medium sized egg yolks
150 ml ($\frac{1}{4}$ pint) double cream

Put the pork fat in the freezer compartment of the refrigerator for 30 minutes.

Have the hare paunched, skinned and the saddle prepared for roasting. Reserve the head, trim off half of the rib-cage and the belly flaps, and use for hare soup (see page 26). Strictly speaking, the saddle only is used for this dish but the upper part of the hind legs can be included to make a young hare serve 6 people.

recipe continues overleaf

Cut the fat into long strips like giant matchsticks and lard the meat in the following way. With a sharp pointed knife pierce the meat of the saddle from tail-end to neck on either side of the back bone. Twist the knife once to form a channel, withdraw it, insert a long strip of fat and push it in fully with a skewer. Make two channels in each thigh along the length and lard them in the same way. Place the saddle and thighs in a deep earthenware dish just large enough to hold them and prepare the marinade.

Peel and coarsely chop the shallots and garlic, peel and finely slice the carrots and onions and strew these vegetables over the hare. Crush the peppercorns and add these to the dish with the herbs. Pour the wine down the sides of the dish: it should just cover the meat. Cover the dish and leave in a cool place for 3 days, turning the meat each day. Do not refrigerate.

Heat the oven to 200°C, 400°F, Gas 6. Peel the grapes and put them into a small dish. Pour the brandy over them, cover and set aside.

Cut the bacon into *lardons* the size of the little finger. Drain the hare, strain and reserve the marinade, place saddle and thighs closely together in a heavy metal baking dish, arrange the *lardons* around them and cover with buttered foil. Roast for 20 minutes, then reduce the heat to 190° C, 375° F, Gas 5, and roast for a further 45 minutes or until the meat is tender when pierced with a sharp knife. Remove the meat and arrange on a heated serving dish with the saddle cut into 4 serving pieces. Cover tightly with foil and put back into the oven with the heat turned off. Put the grapes into the oven to heat through.

Remove the *lardons* from the baking dish, slowly pour off all fat, reserving the meat juices, add 300 ml (½ pint) of the reserved marinade and over low heat scrape up the meat residue from the bottom of the pan with the back of a fork, working it into the juices. Add the brandy from the grapes, season and simmer for a few moments. Beat the egg yolks into the cream and season lightly. Draw the dish from the heat when bubbling fast, add a ladleful of sauce to the cream, beat well and return this mixture slowly to the baking dish stirring constantly. Replace over minimum heat and stir until the sauce thickens slightly. *Do not boil*. Pour the sauce over the hare, garnish with the grapes and serve immediately with boiled rice. Serve the same wine as that used for the marinade.

———————————

Domestic rabbit, as cooked in the French farmhouse kitchen, is a great delicacy. In the Midi, rabbits are fed on sprigs of savory or rosemary to aromatise the flesh.

Meurette de lapin
(Rabbit in Cream Sauce)
Serves 4

1 young rabbit (1.5 kg [3 lb])
12 small onions (pickling size)
100 g (4 oz) butter
1 tablespoon flour
350 ml (12 fl oz) dry white wine
150 ml (¼ pint) water
1 large sprig each thyme and savory or
  rosemary
1 bay leaf
salt, black pepper
3 slices stale bread
2 medium sized egg yolks
200 ml (7 fl oz) double cream
juice 1 small lemon
1 tablespoon chopped parsley

Cut the rabbit into serving pieces, wipe them with a cloth wrung out in cold water and dry well. Peel the onions. Melt 25 g (1 oz) butter in a *sauteuse* or large iron frying pan over low heat and when foaming add the onions and pieces of rabbit, season well and cook slowly until coloured to the blond stage. Sprinkle with flour, mix well and continue cooking for 5 minutes, moving the ingredients about with a wooden spatula so that they do not colour further. Add the wine and water, the herbs tied together and seasoning. Cover and continue simmering until the meat is tender, about 45 minutes.

Remove the crusts from the bread and cut the bread into 2.5 cm (1 inch) wide strips. Heat 60 g (2½ oz) butter in a frying pan until foaming and fry the bread until golden brown and crisp. Drain the *croûtons* on absorbent paper in a hot oven until required.

Put the egg yolks into a small bowl, add the cream, lemon juice, and remaining butter cut into little flecks, beat well and set aside.

To serve, remove the pieces of rabbit and the onions to a heated serving dish with a slotted spoon, cover and keep hot.

Draw the pan from the heat when simmering steadily, add a tablespoon of the cooking liquid to the bowl, stir well and slowly return this mixture to the pan, stirring constantly until the sauce thickens. Pour it over the meat, garnish with the *croûtons* and chopped parsley and serve immediately with small boiled potatoes.

Lapin au chou
(Rabbit with Cabbage)
Serves 4–5

1 young rabbit (1.5 kg [3 lb])
225 g (8 oz) pickled belly of pork (see page 83)
1.2 kg (2½ lb) firm hearted green cabbage
4 medium sized onions
2 carrots
25 g (1 oz) pork dripping
salt, black pepper
150 ml (¼ pint) warm water

Joint the rabbit and cut into serving pieces. Wipe with a cloth wrung out in cold water and dry well. Wash the pickled pork in several changes of cold water, cut into *lardons* the size of the little finger, throw into a pan of boiling water and simmer for 3 minutes, no more. Drain and dry thoroughly. Wash the cabbage, remove and discard any tough outside leaves. Remove the rib from the large edible leaves, quarter the heart and cut out the centre core. Blanch the heart and outside leaves for 5 minutes in boiling water. Drain and set aside. Peel and slice the onions and carrots medium-thick.

Melt the pork dripping in a *sauteuse* or large iron frying pan and colour the pieces of rabbit on both sides to golden brown. As they are browned remove from the pan with a slotted spoon and set aside. Add the *lardons*, lower the heat and colour them to the blond stage. Stir in the onions and carrots and colour all three ingredients until golden brown, stirring frequently.

In a *cocotte* or heavy iron pan place a layer of cabbage, season lightly, cover with pieces of rabbit, a layer of pork and vegetables and so on until the *cocotte* is full, ending with a layer of cabbage and a sprinkling of pork and vegetables. Add the warm water, cover and place over very low heat. When boiling point is reached simmer for about 1 hour 15 minutes, lifting the lid as little as possible. Test with a pointed knife and if there is a great deal of liquid when the meat is tender remove the lid, increase the heat and simmer for a further 10 minutes to reduce.

Serve very hot with potatoes boiled in their skins.

Chapter Nine

VEGETABLES

The extra large globe artichokes grown in Brittany are served with pride in the homes of the growers. For everyday meals they are boiled and served with *vinaigrette* or *sauce au citron* (pages 61 and 80). When visitors are expected the artichokes are prepared in a manner which brings them into the *haute cuisine* class and make an excellent first course for special occasions.

Artichauts barigoule
(Stuffed Artichoke Hearts)
Serves 6

juice 2 lemons
6 large globe artichokes
4 shallots
225 g (8 oz) button mushrooms
150 g (5 oz) streaky bacon (cut in one piece)
1 tablespoon chopped parsley
salt, black pepper, nutmeg
3 tablespoons olive oil
6 large bacon rashers
150 g (5 oz) chopped onion
150 g (5 oz) chopped carrot
150 ml ($\frac{1}{4}$ pint) dry white wine
1 sprig each rosemary and savory or thyme
1 bay leaf

Pour half the lemon juice into a shallow dish. Using a stainless steel knife to prevent discolouration, peel the artichokes raw as potatoes are peeled, removing all the leaves and leaving the heart free but the choke or hairy centre tuft intact. Turn them immediately in the lemon juice to prevent them turning black and place in a large saucepan. Cover barely with cold water, add the rest of the lemon juice and cook over medium heat until half-cooked. Remove the choke by scraping it off with the side of a fork.

Heat the oven to 220°C, 425°F, Gas 7.

Peel the shallots, wipe the mushrooms with a damp cloth and trim the stalks. Remove the rind from the piece of bacon and cut the meat into pieces. Chop these 3 ingredients together finely and add the parsley at the last stage. Season well and add a generous pinch of grated nutmeg.

Pour 1 tablespoon oil into a *sauteuse* and when hot sauté this mixture for about 5 minutes over fairly high heat, stirring frequently and shaking the pan until the contents start to colour. Garnish the artichoke hearts with this preparation, wrap each one in a rasher of bacon, secure with a wooden toothpick and set aside.

Heat the remaining oil in a *cocotte* or heavy braising pan and colour the chopped onion and carrot to the blond stage. Season well, arrange the stuffed hearts on top, pour the wine over them and add the herbs tied together. Cover and cook for 30 minutes in the oven. Uncover and cook for a further 10 minutes to reduce the sauce.

To serve, remove the herbs, place the artichoke hearts in the centre of a heated serving dish and pour the vegetables and sauce around them.

When served as a supper dish *artichauts barigoule* can be served with boiled rice.

The market gardeners of Provence, whose most important crops are aubergines, tomatoes and courgettes, have innumerable ways of cooking their produce, and new recipes are discovered every day. This recipe for aubergines is served at a farm of my acquaintance as a main course on summer evenings. It holds all the savours of the Midi.

Aubergines aux trois fromages
(Aubergines with Three Cheeses)
Serves 4 as a main course

100 g (4 oz) gruyère cheese
75 g (3 oz) Parmesan cheese
175 g (6 oz) curd cheese
1 kg (2 lb) aubergines
salt, black pepper
3–4 tablespoons olive oil
150 g (5 oz) canned tomato purée

Buy the gruyère and Parmesan cheese in whole pieces: they have much more flavour when grated as required. Buy the curd cheese loose from the delicatessen counter: the commercial variety in cartons is not suitable for this recipe.

Wipe the aubergines with a damp cloth, remove the green stem end and peel thinly with a sharp knife. Slice into 5 mm ($\frac{1}{4}$ inch) thick slices, cutting on the slant to make long equal-sized pieces.

Sprinkle liberally with salt and place salt-side down in one layer on a large dinner plate. Sprinkle again with salt and cover with a second slice and so on until all the slices are layered and salted. Place another plate on top and a weight on top of that. Leave for at least 1 hour. Holding the two plates firmly together, squeeze tightly and hold up for the juice to drip away. Wash the slices thoroughly in cold water and dry well.

Heat half the oil in a large frying pan over moderate heat and colour half the aubergines, placed in one layer, until golden on both sides. Remove from the pan. Add more oil and brown the remaining aubergines. Heat the oven to 180°C, 350°F, Gas 4. Grate the gruyère and Parmesan cheese.

Place a layer of aubergines in a shallow oven dish, dot with small pieces of curd cheese, season with pepper, sprinkle with grated gruyère and Parmesan and cover with another layer of aubergines. Repeat until the dish is full, ending with a scattering of gruyère and Parmesan. Empty the tomato purée into a small bowl, fill the can 3 times with hot water, beat this into the purée and pour down the sides of the dish.

Bake for 45 minutes, then increase the heat to 200°C, 400°F, Gas 6, and cook for a further 15 minutes until crusted and bubbling. Serve immediately.

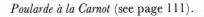

Poularde à la Carnot (see page 111).

122

Aubergines sautées à l'ail
(Aubergines with Garlic)
Serves 4

3 medium sized aubergines
2 cloves garlic
3–4 tablespoons olive oil
salt, black pepper
4 tablespoons chopped parsley

Trim and peel the aubergines and cut into 1 cm ($\frac{1}{2}$ inch) thick slices. Draw off their bitter juices by salting as indicated in the previous recipe. Peel and chop the garlic very finely. Cut the aubergine slices into large cubes, spread them on a thick towel and twist gently to expel the moisture. Pour the oil into a very large frying pan placed over low heat. Arrange the aubergines in one layer in the pan and sauté them, turning over the cubes with a wooden spatula from time to time and shaking the pan so that they cook without colouring too soon. When they reach the blond stage, sprinkle with chopped garlic, salt and plenty of pepper, mix well and cook for 5 minutes. Add the parsley, mix again and cook together until the aubergines are golden brown and the garlic is soft. Serve immediately.

Chou rouge limousin (see page 130), *carottes à l'étuvée* (see page 126), *salade de pommes de terre chaude* (see page 62).

Some of the old French country dishes have very strange names, like the one known as one-eyed *bouillabaisse*. Unlike the true dish of this name, which is made entirely of fish, this one is made of vegetables. It is, however, boiled and then cooked over lowered heat as the word *bouillabaisse* implies. The distinction of being one-eyed comes from the poached egg served on top.

Bouillabaisse borgne
(Vegetable Bouillabaisse)
Serves 4 as a main course

12 walnut halves
4 tablespoons olive oil
2 large leeks
2 medium-large onions
1 clove garlic
4 large Mediterranean tomatoes or 8 large
    domestic tomatoes
peel of $\frac{1}{2}$ small orange
2 sprigs parsley
1 sprig thyme
1 bay leaf
salt, black pepper, saffron
1 litre ($1\frac{3}{4}$ pints) warm water
450 g (1 lb) waxy, red-skinned potatoes
1 tablespoon vinegar
600 ml (1 pint) water
4 large eggs
4 thin slices stale rye bread
1 tablespoon chopped parsley

Grind the walnut halves into the oil with a wooden spoon until crushed small, and set aside. Trim and clean the leeks and cut into short lengths including all edible green parts. Peel the onions and garlic and quarter the onions. Prick the tomatoes in several places, plunge them into boiling water for 1 minute
recipe continues overleaf

and then into cold. Skin and cut each one into 8 sections.

Heat the oil and crushed walnuts in a large pan, add the vegetables and garlic, stir with a wooden spoon to coat with oil and cook over medium heat, stirring frequently, until the onions are coloured to the blond stage. Add the orange peel and the herbs tied together. Season well with salt and pepper, and cover with the warm water. Add a generous pinch of saffron, and stir well. Place over low heat and bring slowly to boiling point. Do not cover. Meanwhile, peel the potatoes and cut into thick slices. If the potatoes are large, halve the slices. Add them to the pan and cook until tender, but do not allow them to disintegrate.

Meanwhile, heat 4 large deep soup-plates. Boil the vinegar and water in a pan and poach the eggs.

To serve, remove the herbs from the *bouillabaisse*, put a slice of bread in the bottom of each plate, ladle the potatoes and vegetables over it and place a poached egg on top. Sprinkle with chopped parsley and serve very hot.

The French enjoy their vegetables and no one more so than the country woman who grows them. She takes a professional pride in creating recipes which preserve all their delicate flavour and these recipes are mostly based on the old principle of cooking vegetables without water.

Carottes à l'étuvée
(Carrots Cooked without Water)
Serves 4

450 g (1 lb) young carrots
2 medium sized onions
15 g ($\frac{1}{2}$ oz) butter
salt, white pepper, sugar
2 tablespoons double cream (optional)

Scrub the carrots, top, tail, scrape them and thinly slice. Peel and chop the onions. Put the butter into a heavy saucepan over low heat and when melting swirl it round to cover the bottom of the pan. Add the onions in a thick layer, sprinkle with salt, arrange the carrots on top, sprinkle with sugar and season lightly. Cover the pan with a sheet of buttered greaseproof paper and force the lid down to seal tightly. Leave over very low heat for 15 minutes, then lift the lid and test with the point of a knife. The carrots should be tender and slightly crisp, having cooked in the steam and moisture made by the tightly closed pan and the onions. If there is any excess moisture raise the heat to medium and shake the pan until the excess is absorbed. Stir in the cream, if used, and serve immediately.

Carottes poulette
(Carrots with Onions in Parsley and Lemon Sauce)
Serve 4

225 g (8 oz) small onions (pickling size)
about 300 ml (½ pint) salted water
450 g (1 lb) young carrots
300 ml (½ pint) milk
15 g (½ oz) butter
1 tablespoon flour
salt, white and black pepper
2 tablespoons chopped parsley
juice ½ lemon
1 large egg yolk

Peel the onions and cook slowly in just enough salted water to cover. Do not boil them fast or they will disintegrate. Drain and reserve the cooking water.

Peel and finely slice the carrots and cook in the milk until tender but still slightly crisp. Drain and reserve the milk.

Melt the butter in a saucepan and work in the flour. Cook them together over low heat for a few moments stirring constantly and then pour in the milk and the onion water, beating constantly with a hand whisk until smooth. Season with a little more salt and some white and black pepper. Bring slowly to boiling point over fairly low heat and when simmering cook for 5 minutes stirring constantly. Mix in the vegetables and the parsley and continue cooking for a further 5 minutes after boiling point returns. Test for seasoning and correct if necessary, then add a few drops of lemon juice at a time until the flavours are sharpened to taste. Draw the pan from the heat, beat in the egg yolk thoroughly, pour into a heated serving dish and serve immediately.

Céleri-rave sauté
(Celeriac with Butter and Lemon)
Serves 4

750 g (1½ lb) celeriac
50 g (2 oz) butter
2 tablespoons corn or olive oil
salt, black pepper
juice 1 lemon
2 tablespoons chopped tarragon or parsley

Peel the celeriac and cut into 2.5 cm (1 inch) thick slices. Cut each slice into 8 or 10 pieces and drop into a panful of fast-boiling salted water. Blanch for 3 minutes only. Drain and pat dry in a cloth. Heat the butter and oil in a large iron frying pan over medium heat and, when the butter froths, arrange the celeriac pieces in the bottom in one layer, season, increase the heat slightly and sauté until golden brown, turning the pieces with a wooden spatula and shaking the pan to prevent sticking.

When ready to serve, sprinkle with lemon juice and chopped herbs. Shake and sauté again, and correct the seasoning if necessary. Turn into a heated serving dish, and serve immediately.

When very large field mushrooms can be found they make a remarkably good dish if cooked with a few good pork sausages or home-made sausagemeat (see page 93).

Champignons à l'ail
(Mushrooms with Garlic and Sausagemeat)
Serves 4 as a supper dish

1 kg (2 lb) open field mushrooms
4–5 large cloves garlic
4 country pork sausages or about 225 g (8 oz)
   home-made sausagemeat
3 tablespoons chopped parsley
salt, black pepper
2 tablespoons olive oil
3 thick slices bread
50 g (2 oz) butter

Wipe the mushrooms with a damp cloth, remove the stalks and peel the caps. Scrape and trim the stalks and chop them. Peel the garlic and chop, then mix in the mushroom stalks and chop them both finely. If using sausages, remove their skins. Add the sausage-meat to the mushroom mixture. Mix in the parsley, season with salt and pepper and mix thoroughly. Heat the oil in a heavy iron casserole and place a layer of mushroom caps in the bottom, open side uppermost. Sprinkle lightly with salt and black pepper. Cover with a layer of *hachis* (the garlic and sausage mixture) and then with another layer of caps. Continue layering with the *hachis* and caps, ending with a layer of *hachis*. Season lightly, cover the casserole with a sheet of buttered greaseproof paper, sprinkle a few drops of cold water on top and force the lid of the casserole down to seal tightly. Place over very low heat and cook as gently as possible for 1½ hours. Lift the lid only at 30-minute intervals, adding 1 or 2 tablespoons water when the mushroom juices have been absorbed.

Meanwhile, remove the crusts from the bread and cut the bread into 2.5 cm (1 inch) wide strips. Heat the butter in a frying pan until foaming and fry the bread until golden brown and crisp. Drain on kitchen paper in a hot oven until required.

To serve, stand the *croûtons* around the inside of the casserole and serve immediately.

The country cooking of France can transform even cabbage into a gourmet's dish by cooking it without water. Any cabbage can be cooked in this way—white or green—but it must have a tight, firm heart.

Chou à la paysanne
(Cabbage with Leeks and Onions)
Serves 4

1 kg (2 lb) firm hearted cabbage
1 large onion
1 large leek
25 g (1 oz) butter or pork fat
salt, white pepper
1 tablespoon chopped mint

Wash and trim the cabbage, remove tough outer leaves and quarter the heart. Remove the inside core leaving just enough to hold the leaves together and cut each quarter into 1 cm (½ inch) thick slices. Peel and coarsely chop the onion, trim and clean the leek, removing the dark green part of the leaves which can be used for soup. Slice the white and pale green parts.

Thickly coat a heavy iron casserole with half the butter or pork fat and put the chopped onion in the bottom in one layer, season well with salt and lightly with pepper. Next add the slices of cabbage, packing them in tightly in one layer, season lightly and cover with the sliced leek, season and dot with the rest of the butter or pork fat. Cover the casserole with a sheet of buttered greaseproof paper, sprinkle a few drops of cold water on top and force the lid of the casserole down to seal tightly. Place over fairly low heat for 3 minutes until the contents start to bubble, then reduce the heat to minimum and cook for 15 minutes before lifting the lid. Test with a pointed knife. The cabbage should remain slightly crisp when cooked. Scatter the chopped mint on top and serve very hot in the casserole. As an alternative flavouring, omit the mint and scatter 1 teaspoon caraway seeds over the layer of cabbage before covering with leeks.

Breton farmers grow large crops of potatoes and onions and their wives have numerous ways of cooking them. Combined with cabbage they make an interesting vegetable dish.

Chou à la bretonne
(Cabbage with Potatoes)
Serves 4

750 g (1½ lb) firm hearted cabbage
350 g (12 oz) floury potatoes
225 g (8 oz) onions
salt, black and white pepper
50 g (2 oz) butter
2 tablespoons chopped chives or spring onion
    tops

Wash and trim the cabbage, remove tough outer leaves and quarter the heart. Remove the inside core leaving just enough to hold the leaves together and cut each quarter into 1 cm (½ inch) thick slices.

Peel and quarter the potatoes and onions and place them in a panful of lightly salted cold water. Bring to boiling point over medium heat and boil for 10 minutes. Add the sliced cabbage and cook for a further 10 minutes until the cabbage is only just tender, still slightly crisp, and the other vegetables are soft. Drain well, press out excess moisture gently with a saucer. Shake well and replace the pan over low heat to dry the contents. Season well, add the butter cut into small pieces, scatter the herbs on top and carefully turn the vegetables over with two forks until the cabbage is shining and buttery. Serve very hot.

In the farms of the Limousin area this very good dish of red cabbage is made in large quantity because it is almost better when reheated than when cooked the first time. On special occasions it is served with roast pork, for family meals with grilled sausages.

Chou rouge limousin
(Red Cabbage with Chestnuts and Red Wine)
Serves 8–10

1.5 kg (3 lb) red cabbage
100 g (4 oz) pickled belly of pork (see page 83)
1 medium sized onion
200 ml (7 fl oz) red wine
2 tablespoons wine vinegar
½ teaspoon each salt, ground cloves
nutmeg
1 kg (2 lb) chestnuts (fresh or canned and unsweetened)

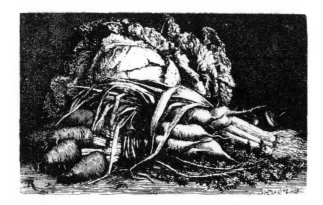

Wash and trim the cabbage, remove tough outer leaves and quarter the heart. Remove inside core and shred cabbage finely. Wash the pickled pork in several changes of cold water, cut into *lardons* the size of the little finger, throw into a pan of boiling water and simmer for 5 minutes. Drain and dry thoroughly. Peel and coarsely chop the onion. Heat a large iron *cocotte* over low heat for a few moments and sauté the *lardons*. Move them about with a wooden spatula until they render their fat and are coloured golden brown on all sides. Remove with a slotted spoon and set aside.

Add the onion, mix into the rendered fat and brown lightly, then add the cabbage and mix thoroughly. Cover and cook over low heat for 10 minutes. Add the *lardons*, wine, vinegar, salt, cloves and a pinch of grated nutmeg. Mix again, cover and cook over minimum heat for 2 hours.

If using fresh chestnuts, heat the oven to 240 °C, 475 °F, Gas 9. Slit the skin of the chestnuts on the rounded side. Place them in a baking tin, spread out, add 1 cm (½ inch) water, put the tin in the oven and bake for about 10 minutes. The chestnuts must not brown at all, but by this time their 2 skins should peel off easily. If not, cover with a wet cloth and set aside for a few minutes, then peel. If tinned chestnuts are used, drain them well.

Add the chestnuts to the cabbage after it has cooked for 2 hours. Stir them in, correct the seasoning, adding a little more vinegar, salt or spices if necessary, cover and cook for 1 hour longer. This dish must cook slowly at all times. It can be cooked in a casserole in the oven at 170°C, 325°F, Gas 3, after being prepared in a heavy iron frying pan.

To reheat, set the oven at 190°C, 375°F, Gas 5, put the remainder into an earthenware dish, cover tightly with foil and place it in a baking tin half full of boiling water. Heat in the oven for about 30 minutes.

Choux de Bruxelles au gratin
(Brussels Sprouts with Cheese Sauce)
Serves 4 as a supper dish

300 ml ($\frac{1}{2}$ pint) *béchamel* sauce (see following
    recipe)
1 kg (2 lb) small brussels sprouts
50 g (2 oz) butter
salt, black pepper, nutmeg
75 g (3 oz) gruyère cheese
4 tablespoons double cream

Make the *béchamel* sauce as instructed and set
it aside.

Trim the brussels sprouts and cut a cross
into the root end so that this tougher part
cooks quickly. Wash under cold running
water and throw into a panful of boiling
salted water. Cook until barely tender, drain,
press lightly with the rounded side of a saucer
to expel as much moisture as possible and
shake to separate again. Melt the butter in a
large iron frying pan over low heat and when
foaming sauté the sprouts, tossing them and
shaking the pan until they are dry. Do not
allow to colour. Season well with salt, pepper
and grated nutmeg, mix in half the *béchamel*
and pour into a buttered *gratin* dish. Grate the
cheese and mix half of it, and the cream, into
the rest of the sauce and pour over the sprouts.
Scatter the remainder of the cheese on top and
place under a preheated grill to crisp and
brown. Serve immediately.

Sauce béchamel
(Béchamel Sauce)

Makes 300 ml ($\frac{1}{2}$ pint)

15 g ($\frac{1}{2}$ oz) butter
2 teaspoons flour
300 ml ($\frac{1}{2}$ pint) hot milk
salt, black pepper

Makes 600 ml (1 pint)

25 g (1 oz) butter
1 tablespoon flour
600 ml (1 pint) hot milk
salt, black pepper

Melt the butter in a small saucepan over low
heat and work in the flour with a wooden
spoon. Cook together for a few moments without allowing the mixture to colour and then
add the hot milk, gradually stirring until
incorporated (hot milk prevents lumps from
forming). Increase the heat to moderate and
simmer for 5 minutes after boiling point is
reached, stirring meanwhile, until the sauce is
thick and smooth.

If the sauce has to wait before use, cover
with a piece of buttered paper pressed lightly
on to the surface. This will prevent a skin from
forming.

If the sauce is required in a hurry the milk
can be added cold but, in this case, the pan
must be removed from the heat when the
butter and flour are cooked and the milk
added all at once, beating constantly. Then,
when the mixture is smooth, return the pan to
the heat and cook as indicated previously.

Small, delicately flavoured courgettes make an appetising and most attractive first course or light lunch dish when stuffed and served either hot or cold.

Courgettes farcies
(Stuffed Courgettes)
Serves 6

12 small courgettes
1 thick slice white bread
100 ml (4 fl oz) milk
175 g (6 oz) home-made sausagemeat (see
   page 93) or lean cold meat, finely chopped
salt, black pepper, nutmeg
1 tablespoon chopped parsley
2 tablespoons olive oil
2 medium sized onions
350 g (12 oz) tomatoes
chapelure (see page 67)
25 g (1 oz) butter

Wipe the courgettes with a damp cloth. Remove top and tail-ends. Plunge them into boiling salted water and simmer gently for 5 minutes. Drain well and set aside. Heat the oven to 200°C, 400°F, Gas 6. Soak the bread in the milk until soft then squeeze out excess moisture and crumble it into the meat. Season well with salt, pepper and a generous pinch of nutmeg. Add the chopped parsley and mix well. Slice the courgettes into halves lengthways, scoop out a little of the flesh with a teaspoon, chop it and add to the meat mixture. Pour half the oil into a large *gratin* dish and rub it round to coat all surfaces. Arrange the courgettes in one layer in the dish, cut side uppermost, and season.

Peel and finely chop the onion. Prick the tomatoes in several places, plunge them into boiling water for 1 minute and then into cold. Skin, cut into halves, remove the seeds with a teaspoon, chop the flesh roughly and mix with the onion. Heat the rest of the oil in a small frying pan and in it cook the onion mixture until soft. Season well, then stir in the meat

mixture and cook together slowly—for 10 to 15 minutes if sausagemeat is used, for 5 minutes if cold meat is used.

Fill the courgettes with this preparation, piling it up high to cover the surface. Scatter thickly with *chapelure* and dot with little flecks of butter. Bake for 20 minutes until the courgettes are tender when pierced with a pointed knife and the top is well browned.

Small tomatoes can be halved horizontally, scooped out and filled with the same mixture. Do not peel them and do not blanch them in boiling water before filling and baking.

A dish of mixed stuffed courgettes and tomatoes makes an enticing display.

Provençal people serve the following dish of courgettes accompanied by plain boiled rice as a main course in place of meat.

Courgettes provençale
(Courgettes with Tomatoes, Cheese and Garlic)
Serves 4

4 large Mediterranean tomatoes or 8 large
   domestic tomatoes
1 medium sized onion
750 g (1½ lb) courgettes
2 cloves garlic
2 tablespoons olive oil
¼ teaspoon dried thyme
salt, black pepper
2 tablespoons chopped parsley
100 g (4 oz) gruyère cheese
15 g (½ oz) butter
4 tablespoons dry white wine
chapelure (see page 67)

Prick the tomatoes in several places, plunge them into boiling water for 1 minute and then into cold. Skin, cut into halves, remove the seeds with a teaspoon and chop the flesh roughly. Peel and chop the onion. Peel the courgettes and cut into thick slices. Peel and crush the garlic and put it into a large frying pan with the oil over gentle heat. Place one layer of courgettes in the pan and cook just long enough to soften slightly. Do not over-cook. Lift out of the pan with a slotted spoon and keep warm. Half-cook the rest in the same way. In the same oil cook the onion and when it starts to soften add the tomato flesh and thyme, mix well and cook for about 30 minutes until reduced to a thick consistency. Season well and stir in the chopped parsley. Heat the oven to 200°C, 400°F, Gas 6. Grate the cheese.

Butter a shallow ovenproof dish and place half the courgettes in it in one layer. Season and cover with half the cheese and half the tomato mixture, cover with the rest of the courgettes, cheese and tomatoes. Pour the wine down the sides of the dish, sprinkle the surface thickly with *chapelure* and bake for 30 to 40 minutes until bubbling and brown on top. Serve immediately with boiled rice.

A heavy crop of courgettes poses a problem to the market gardener's wife. She is expected to utilise the surplus when the main crop has been sold. After cooking them with every recipe she knows the rest are preserved. In this way they remain fresh for at least two months, to be relished as an *hors d'oeuvre* long after their natural season is over.

Courgettes à la sauge
(Marinated Courgettes)
Serve as a first course

1.5 kg (3 lb) medium-small courgettes
6–7 tablespoons olive oil
salt, black pepper

2 cloves garlic
6 large sage leaves
300 ml (½ pint) red wine vinegar
350 ml (12 fl oz) dry white wine

Wash and dry the courgettes. Remove top and tail-ends and then cut into thick slanting slices down the length. Heat 3 tablespoons oil in a very large iron frying pan over medium heat and in one layer at a time quickly sauté the slices to the golden stage on both sides. Do not cook through or colour deeply. Set them aside on a plate when sautéd until all have been dealt with, adding another tablespoon of oil to the pan if necessary.

Layer the courgettes in a long rectangular *pâté* dish, seasoning each layer. Empty the pan of any remaining oil and wipe it clean with kitchen paper. Pour in 3 tablespoons olive oil. Peel the garlic and add to the pan with the sage leaves. Cook slowly until the garlic is golden coloured. Pour in the vinegar and wine and simmer slowly for a few moments. When boiling hot pour over the courgettes to cover, push the garlic cloves down the sides of the dish and arrange the sage leaves on top. When cold, cover with foil and refrigerate.

If a stronger garlic flavour is preferred, chop the peeled garlic together with the sage leaves and sprinkle a little of this mixture, raw, between the layers of sautéd courgettes. Heat the fresh oil, vinegar and wine until boiling, beat well and pour immediately over the courgettes.

To serve, remove about 6 slices per person from the dish 1 hour before required and serve with thin slices of buttered rye bread and the same wine as that used in the recipe.

All French vegetables are picked very small and tender, when their flavour is at its best. This explains why they are served as a separate course in France. Broad beans especially must be very young to be cooked in the following way.

Fèves en chemise
(Broad Beans in Tarragon Sauce)
Serves 4

1 kg (2 lb) young broad beans
600 ml (1 pint) *béchamel* sauce (see page 131)
2 tablespoons chopped tarragon or parsley
juice ½ lemon
salt, black pepper
1 large egg yolk

Wash the beans quickly under cold running water and snip off the top and tail. They should be too young to have side strings. Cut the whole pod into short lengths including the beans inside and cook rapidly in boiling water for about 10 minutes. Do not add salt; it makes them tough. Cook until barely tender, bearing in mind that they will be cooked later for a further 2 or 3 minutes. Drain and set aside.

Make the sauce as advised, and add the chopped herb and lemon juice to taste. Season the beans with salt and pepper and mix them into the sauce. Stir carefully and when boiling point is reached simmer together over low heat for a few minutes. Test for seasoning and add a few more drops of lemon juice if necessary. Remove the pan from the heat, stir in the egg yolk until incorporated, and pour into a heated serving dish.

Very young broad beans cooked with herbs and cream are excellent served with a thick slice of cold boiled ham.

Fèves à la crème
(Broad Beans with Cream and Herbs)
Serves 4

1 kg (2 lb) young broad beans
40 g (1½ oz) butter
salt, black pepper
2 tablespoons chopped chervil, tarragon, savory or chives
4 tablespoons double cream

Shell the beans and cook in just enough boiling salted water to cover. When just tender, drain, and put the dry pan back over medium heat. Melt the butter, add the beans, season well, and sauté them for a few minutes. That is, toss the beans in the butter and shake the pan over the heat so that the contents do not colour. Add the herbs, sauté again to mix well and stir in the cream carefully. Correct the seasoning if necessary and when thoroughly hot, pour into a heated serving dish and serve immediately.

Fèves à la crème aigre
(Broad Beans with Sour Cream)
Serves 4

1 kg (2 lb) broad beans
1 clove garlic
150 ml (¼ pint) sour cream
1 teaspoon strong French mustard
1 teaspoon lemon juice
1 teaspoon grated lemon rind

1 tablespoon chopped tarragon or mint
salt, black pepper, nutmeg
1 teaspoon brown sugar (optional)
1 large egg yolk

Shell the beans and cook in just enough salted water to cover. Drain them well and keep hot. Peel and crush the garlic and mix into the sour cream with the mustard, lemon juice and rind, chopped tarragon or mint, seasoning, and the sugar if used. Pour this mixture into the hot pan and place over low heat. Add the beans and when the first bubble rises draw the pan from the heat, beat in the egg yolk and stir thoroughly to blend. Pour into a heated serving dish and serve immediately.

———————————————

The fineness of French green beans (*haricots verts*) is unbelievable and so is the price of those imported into this country. Our own runner beans, if picked *very* young, when not more than 10 cm (4 inches) long, can be a good substitute when cooked in the farmhouse manner. This is a good vegetable dish to serve with grilled chops.

Haricots verts à la tomate
(Green Beans with Tomatoes)
Serves 4

450 g (1 lb) very small runner beans or other
   green beans
350 g (12 oz) large tomatoes (preferably
  Mediterranean variety)
40 g (1½ oz) butter
salt, black pepper, paprika
4 tablespoons double cream

Wash the beans quickly under cold running water and snip off the top and tail. They should be too young to have side strings. Cook for 8 to 10 minutes in a pan of boiling salted water. Meanwhile, prick the tomatoes in several places, plunge them into boiling water for 1 minute and then into cold. Skin, cut into halves, remove the seeds with a teaspoon and chop the flesh roughly. Melt the butter in another pan, add the tomatoes, season well and cook over medium heat. Do not cover the pan.

Drain the beans well and add to the tomatoes, mix carefully and cook until the beans are tender but still slightly crisp. Stir in the cream, add a generous pinch of paprika, test for seasoning, correct if necessary, and heat without boiling.

Serve immediately.

———————————————

Braised chestnuts served whole, tender and glossy, make a fitting accompaniment to roast pheasant or roast pork.

Marrons braisés
(Braised Chestnuts)
Serves 4

1 kg (2 lb) chestnuts
3 branches celery
40 g (1½ oz) butter
1 teaspoon sugar
salt, black pepper

Skin the chestnuts as advised in recipe on page 110. Chop the celery finely. Melt the butter in a wide based pan or *sauteuse* and place the chestnuts in it in one layer. Shake the pan to coat them with butter and add sufficient warm water to barely cover them.

Sprinkle with sugar, add the chopped celery, salt and pepper. Place over low heat and bring slowly to boiling point. Cover and simmer slowly for about 45 minutes. Drain off any remaining liquid and serve immediately.

In days gone by when small holding farmers throughout France lived on a diet in which chestnuts figured largely, this replacement for potatoes was cooked in an infinite number of ways. Times are now prosperous for French farmers but they still regard chestnuts as a good dish for supper when cooked with onions and wine in a casserole.

Ragoût de marrons
(Chestnuts and Onions in White Wine)
Serves 4 as a supper dish

1.5 kg (3 lb) chestnuts
8 small onions (pickling size)
4 shallots
50 g (2 oz) butter
300 ml (½ pint) dry white wine
150 ml (¼ pint) *bouillon*
salt, black pepper

Skin the chestnuts as advised in recipe on page 110. Peel the onions and leave them whole. Peel and chop the shallots finely.

Melt the butter in a wide-based pan or *sauteuse* over low heat and when foaming add the shallots and cook slowly until soft without colouring. Carefully stir in the chestnuts to coat with melted butter and spread them out in the bottom of the pan. Place the small onions in between and pour the wine and *bouillon* over them. The liquid should barely cover them. Season with salt and plenty of pepper, cover, and cook slowly for about 45 minutes. The chestnuts must be slowly cooked at all times so that they do not fall apart. Remove the chestnuts and onions with a slotted spoon to a heated serving dish, cover and keep hot. Increase the heat and reduce the sauce slightly to thicken a little and pour it boiling hot over the chestnuts and onions. Serve immediately.

Young purple-skinned turnips pulled when very small are regarded as a delicacy by French country people. Amateur gardeners in this country who are producing fine crops of turnips will be interested in the recipe used to present this much neglected vegetable at its best.

Navets à la crème
(Young Turnips with Cream)
Serves 4

750 g (1½ lb) very small turnips
salt, black pepper
75 g (3 oz) butter
6 tablespoons double cream

Peel the turnips. Cut into halves horizontally if very small, if medium-small cut into thick slices. Place in a *sauteuse* or wide based pan in one layer with just sufficient cold water to barely cover them. Add salt, cover, place over medium heat and cook for 10 minutes. Remove the lid, stir in the butter cut into small pieces and continue cooking until the water evaporates and the turnips are coloured to the golden stage. During this time baste the turnips occasionally and move them around with a wooden spatula so that they colour on all sides. Add a little salt and some pepper and stir in the cream. When boiling point is reached allow to bubble for a few moments and pour into a heated serving dish. Serve very hot.

Sundays on a French farm mean that an especially good lunch can be expected. No work in the afternoon gives plenty of time to enjoy a first course, as well as a sweet dish for those inclined, both of them treats not indulged in at weekday meals. Vegetable first courses are very popular and those prepared with onions of any variety are regarded as being the most appetising.

Oignons à l'orientale
(Spiced Onions)
Serve as a first course

1 kg (2 lb) small silver-skinned onions or
    pickling onions
salt, black pepper, saffron
about 300 ml ($\frac{1}{2}$ pint) dry white wine
about 4 tablespoons olive oil
1 clove garlic
6 grains coriander
3 large Mediterranean tomatoes or 6 large
    domestic tomatoes

Peel the onions, arrange in one layer in a large wide-based pan or a *sauteuse* and sprinkle with salt. Beat the wine and oil together until cloudy and pour over the onions to barely cover them. Add more if necessary. Peel and finely chop the garlic, crush the coriander. Prick the tomatoes in several places, plunge them into boiling water for 1 minute and then into cold. Skin, cut into halves, remove the seeds with a teaspoon and chop the flesh roughly. Spread the tomatoes over the onions. Season well with salt and pepper, the garlic and coriander, and two generous pinches of saffron. This last should be the predominating flavour. Cover, place over low heat and when boiling reduce the heat to minimum and cook until the onions are tender when pierced with a pointed knife. Leave until cold, pour into a large screw-topped jar and store in the refrigerator.

To serve, drain the number required, about 5 for each person, and serve chilled with thin slices of buttered rye bread.

Petits oignons en vinaigrette
(Spring Onions in French Dressing)
Serves 4–5

3 bunches spring onions
1 tablespoon olive oil
1 tablespoon capers
2 hard-boiled eggs
salt and pepper
4 tablespoons *vinaigrette* (see page 61)

Wash the onions, cut off the root and trim down the green part so that they measure about 10 cm (4 inches). Tie into 5 or 6 little bundles and place them side by side in a *sauteuse* or large frying pan. Pour over just enough cold water to half cover, add the olive oil, cover and place over medium heat. When boiling reduce the heat and steam for about 5 minutes or until tender. Drain well and leave to cool. Drain and chop the capers finely, peel and finely chop the eggs. Untie the bundles of onions and place them head to tail on a serving dish. Season with salt and pepper. Mix the capers into the *vinaigrette* and pour evenly over the onions. Scatter the chopped egg on top and chill slightly before serving with hot French bread.

Making the most of good simple ingredients is one of the gifts of the farmhouse cook. This is the dish with which she regales the farm workers when the leek crop is in full season.

Poireaux à la fermière
(Leeks with Pork in Red Wine)
Serves 6 as a main course

20 medium sized leeks
750 g (1½ lb) lean pickled belly of pork (see page 83)
white pepper, cayenne, ground cloves
600 ml (1 pint) red wine
200 ml (7 fl oz) water
12 thick slices smoked sausage
15 g (½ oz) butter
2 tablespoons breadcrumbs
2 tablespoons chopped parsley
1 large egg yolk

Trim the leeks but remove only the dark green leaves. Retain the pale green part, leaving them whole, and wash thoroughly. Cut the pickled pork into thick slices, place them in a heavy iron casserole. Pour boiling water over, simmer for 5 minutes, drain thoroughly and rearrange in one layer in the casserole. Put the leeks on top in one layer, head to tail, sprinkle with pepper, a little cayenne and a generous pinch of ground cloves. There is no need to add salt, the pickled pork will be salt enough. Mix the wine with the water and pour this down the sides of the dish. Cover the casserole with a sheet of buttered greaseproof paper and force the lid down to seal tightly. Simmer over very gentle heat for 1½ hours without removing the lid.

While the leeks are cooking, sauté the sausage slices in butter and then dip them into the breadcrumbs and parsley mixed together. Heat the oven to 190°C, 375°F, Gas 5.

When the leeks and pork are cooked, lift them out of the casserole with two fish slices without disturbing the layers, if possible, and arrange in a shallow ovenproof dish. Pour the liquid into a bowl and remove all fat first with a metal cooking spoon and then with bands of kitchen paper passed over the surface of the liquid until it is quite clear. Beat the egg yolk in another bowl and add 175 ml (6 fl oz) liquid, beating it in a little at a time. Add seasoning only if necessary and pour this binding over the leeks. Garnish with the cooked sausage rings, scatter the rest of the breadcrumbs and parsley over them and bake for about 20 to 30 minutes until well browned and crusted on top.

Serve with thin slices of rye or wholemeal bread.

Gratin de poireaux
(Leeks with Gruyère Cheese and Bacon)
Serves 4

750 g (1½ lb) medium sized leeks
175 g (6 oz) lean bacon rashers
175 g (6 oz) gruyère cheese
15 g (½ oz) butter
salt, black pepper
250 ml (8 fl oz) chicken *bouillon*

Trim the leeks, removing any damaged leaves but retaining all edible green parts. Slash them down and crossways as far as the white part and plunge them up and down cut-end foremost in a bowl of warm water to remove the grit. When clean, wash in cold water and cut into 5 cm (2 inch) lengths. Blanch in boiling salted water over low heat for about 10 minutes until not quite cooked. Drain well and, when cool, squeeze out all excess moisture. Heat the oven to 180°C, 350°F, Gas 4.

Remove the rind from the bacon and chop the bacon coarsely. Grate the cheese. Coat a *gratin* or other ovenproof dish with the butter, arrange a layer of leeks in the bottom and season lightly. Sprinkle with cheese and scraps of bacon and cover with another layer of leeks. Fill the dish in this way and sprinkle the remaining cheese over the surface.

Pour the *bouillon* down the sides of the dish and bake for about 35 minutes until the leeks are tender and the cheese crusted and browned on top. Serve immediately.

Workers on the coastal farms of northern France, like the mine workers inland, greatly enjoy eating crisply fried sprats with this especially savoury potato dish.

Pommes de terre de la Bassée
(Braised Potatoes and Onions with Garlic)
Serves 6

3 large onions
6 large potatoes
2 tablespoons beef dripping or pork fat
4 cloves garlic
salt, black pepper
1 teaspoon dried thyme

Peel the onions and cut into halves horizontally. Scrub the potatoes but do not peel; cut them into halves lengthways. Melt the dripping or pork fat in a heavy iron *cocotte* and when hot brown the cut side of the potatoes and onions. Add the garlic, peeled but not crushed, season well with salt and pepper, and sprinkle with thyme. Cover the *cocotte* with a sheet of buttered greaseproof paper, sprinkle a few drops of cold water on top and force down the lid to seal tightly. Reduce the heat to very low and cook for about 45 minutes without lifting the lid.

To serve, place the potatoes cut side uppermost on a hot serving dish and arrange the browned onions and garlic around them. Serve immediately.

The combination of hot potatoes and a cool green salad is a delicious one that is served frequently for supper in French farmhouses. Many of these potato recipes have been chosen with this combination in mind.

Pommes de terre au lard
(Potato Casserole with Bacon)
Serves 4

225 g (8 oz) lean streaky bacon (in one piece)
1 medium sized onion
1 clove garlic
450 g (1 lb) large tomatoes (preferably
   Mediterranean variety)
1 kg (2 lb) potatoes
15 g ($\frac{1}{2}$ oz) butter
1 sprig each thyme, rosemary
1 bay leaf
300 ml ($\frac{1}{2}$ pint) *bouillon*
salt and pepper
2 teaspoons flour (optional)
1 tablespoon water (optional)

Remove the rind from the bacon and cut the meat into *lardons* the size of the little finger. Peel and chop the onion coarsely. Peel and finely chop the garlic. Prick the tomatoes in several places, plunge them into boiling water for 1 minute, then into cold, and skin. Peel the potatoes, cut into thick slices and leave in cold water until required. Melt the butter in a heavy pan over low heat and when foaming add the *lardons* and sauté until they start to colour. Add the onions and cook until both are golden brown. Add the tomatoes and cook together for 5 minutes stirring constantly. Add the herbs tied together, the *bouillon*, garlic and potatoes and season well. Increase the heat to medium and cook briskly until the potatoes are tender. Remove the herbs before serving, and test for seasoning. Correct if necessary.

If floury potatoes are used they will most likely have thickened the sauce slightly of themselves. If not, mix the flour and water until smooth, stir into the sauce, reduce the heat and simmer slowly for 5 minutes.

Serve very hot with plenty of crisp French bread.

Pommes de terre à la crème
(Browned Potatoes with Cheese)
Serves 4

1 kg (2 lb) medium sized potatoes
75 g (3 oz) butter
salt, black pepper
75 g (3 oz) Parmesan cheese
150 ml ($\frac{1}{4}$ pint) cream

Peel the potatoes and slice thinly. Wrap in a damp cloth until required. Heat a very large iron frying pan, dry, over medium heat for a few moments. Drop in half the butter and when it foams swirl it round the pan and draw the pan off the heat. Arrange the potatoes in layers, adding seasoning and the rest of the butter cut into small pieces in between each layer. Press down firmly with a wooden spoon and season the top layer. Replace the pan over low heat and colour the potatoes to the golden stage on the underside, shaking the pan frequently to avoid sticking. Reduce the heat and cover to cook the potatoes through. Grate the cheese. Heat the grill at high temperature.

When the potatoes are easily pierced with a pointed knife, increase the heat to crisp the undercrust, push a palette knife underneath, shake the pan to free the contents and slide them on to a heated serving plate, crusted side underneath. Scatter half the cheese over the surface, pour on the cream evenly and cover with the rest of the cheese. Place under the grill to melt and brown. Serve immediately.

Tarte frangipane aux cerises (see page 158).

Pommes de terre à la dauphinoise is a most delectable potato dish of which every French cook, country woman or town dweller, has her version. The ingredients do not differ, it is the manner of putting them together that varies. One thing they all have in common is the crisp golden crust called a *gratin*. In some dishes it is formed with toasted crumbs, either plain, buttered, or mixed with cheese, and scattered over the ingredients before they are baked; it can also be grated cheese as on top of a good onion soup; or it can be the ingredients themselves that form a crisp crust when baked, as in the following recipe.

Pommes de terre à la dauphinoise
(Potatoes Baked in Cream with Cheese)
Serves 4

750 g (1½ lb) waxy, red-skinned potatoes
1 clove garlic
15 g (½ oz) butter
75 g (3 oz) gruyère cheese
400 ml (¾ pint) milk
salt, black pepper, nutmeg
4 tablespoons single cream

Heat the oven to 150°C, 300°F, Gas 2.

Peel and slice the potatoes thinly and wrap in a wet cloth until required. Cut the garlic into halves and rub these round a large *gratin* dish or other shallow ovenproof dish. Butter the dish thickly and set it aside. Grate the cheese.

Put the milk and potatoes and a little salt into a large saucepan over medium heat and

when boiling reduce the heat and cook for 5 minutes. Drain, and reserve the milk. Arrange the potatoes in layers in the dish, seasoning each layer before covering with cream and grated cheese. Before seasoning the last layer pour half the milk over the potatoes and scatter with the remaining cheese. Bake for about 1½ hours, adding the rest of the milk down the sides of the dish until it is all absorbed. Serve in the *gratin* dish.

Until quite recently every tiny hamlet in the high mountains of Savoy had its *four banal*. This community oven was stoked by the villagers who each brought their contribution of wood in return for which they enjoyed the privilege of baking the family's weekly batch of bread. No matter how large the batch, room was always found for a *gratin de pommes de terre à la savoyarde*, a very palatable potato dish, different to its sophisticated relative *à la dauphinoise* but just as good. It is still a popular dish in this region, although the *four banal* may now be more difficult to find.

Pommes de terre à la savoyarde
(Potatoes Baked with Cheese)
Serves 4

750 g (1½ lb) waxy, red-skinned potatoes
150 g (5 oz) gruyère cheese
2 tablespoons flour
salt, black pepper, nutmeg
1 clove garlic
25 g (1 oz) butter
400 ml (¾ pint) chicken *bouillon*
recipe continues overleaf

Bûche flambante (see page 162).

Heat the oven to 150°C, 300°F, Gas 2.

Peel the potatoes and wash and dry them. Grate the cheese. Scatter the flour on a dry pastry board and season well with salt, pepper and grated nutmeg. Slice the potatoes thinly and dry them thoroughly, spread out on a kitchen cloth. Turn them on to the seasoned flour and mix with the hands until coated.

Cut the garlic into halves and rub these round a large *gratin* dish or other shallow ovenproof dish. Coat the dish with half the butter and place a layer of potatoes in the bottom, scatter with grated cheese and cover with another layer of potatoes. Fill the dish in this way, arranging the last layer of potatoes in overlapping rows. Pour the *bouillon* over them, scatter the rest of the cheese evenly over the surface and dot with the rest of the butter cut into little pieces. Place in the lower half of the oven and bake for 1½ hours until well browned and crisp on top. Serve immediately.

The kind of cottage or curd cheese that is required for the following old country recipe is that sold in bulk at delicatessen counters. The processed variety sold in cartons is not suitable.

Le Petatou
(Soufflé Potatoes with Curd Cheese)
Serves 4

450 g (1 lb) floury potatoes
2 large eggs
salt, black pepper
50 g (2 oz) butter
100 g (4 oz) curd cheese

Peel the potatoes and cut into halves. Boil in salted water until tender when pierced with a knife. Meanwhile, separate the eggs. Add a pinch of salt to the egg whites and beat until a stiff peak is formed. Put aside until required. Heat the oven to 200°C, 400°F, Gas 6.

Drain the potatoes, put them into a heated mixing bowl, season highly with salt and pepper, add the butter cut into small pieces and mix thoroughly. Mash down with a potato masher until no lumps remain, add the cottage cheese and beat vigorously until quite smooth. Beat in the egg yolks, test for seasoning and correct if necessary. Beat the egg whites again until very stiff and fold into the potato mixture with an up-and-over movement so that the whites are folded, not beaten or stirred in.

Pour into a shallow buttered oven dish and bake until well risen and golden brown on top, about 20 to 25 minutes. Serve without delay.

Many small children in the goose-farming regions of France start their working life guarding the vast herds of geese and driving them from one good pasture to another prior to fattening. The very young and the very old share this task, all of them sustained no doubt by thoughts of the many gastronomic treats the herd will eventually provide.

One of those treats prepared by the parsimonious farmer's wife is made with the vegetables left over from cooking the goose (see recipe on page 110).

Régal de pommes de terre
(Potatoes in White Wine)
Serves 6

reserved vegetables (see above)
300 ml ($\frac{1}{2}$ pint) white wine
6 medium sized potatoes
$\frac{1}{4}$ litre (8 fl oz) water
salt, black pepper
6 large eggs
1 tablespoon wine vinegar
600 ml (1 pint) salted water
1 tablespoon chopped parsley

Place the reserved vegetables in a heavy iron *cocotte* or large pan and mix in the wine. Peel the potatoes, cut into thick slices and bury them in the vegetables. Add the water, a little salt and pepper and cook, uncovered, over medium heat until the potatoes are tender and the liquid mostly evaporated. Test for seasoning and correct if necessary.

Meanwhile poach the eggs in the vinegar and salted water. Pour the *régal* into a heated dish, arrange the eggs on top, scatter with chopped parsley and serve immediately.

Crisp radishes served with good butter and fresh bread are a favourite appetiser on French tables at lunchtime. When the supply threatens to outstrip demand, rather than allow the radishes to grow large and hollow, the country people cook them and serve them as a hot vegetable.

Radis au beurre à la vapeur
(Steamed Buttered Radishes)
Serves 4

4 bunches firm radishes
2 medium sized onions
50 g (2 oz) butter
salt, black pepper

Remove leaves and roots from the radishes and wash quickly under cold running water. Do not allow them to soak. Peel and coarsely chop the onions.

Melt half the butter in a wide-based pan in which the radishes can eventually be placed in one layer. When the butter foams add the onions, season well and sauté over low heat, shaking the pan so that they soften without colouring. Add the radishes and turn over the mixture with a wooden spoon. Pour into the pan just enough cold water to cover the bottom, cover with a well-fitting lid and cook for 5 minutes, no more. Add the rest of the butter cut into small pieces, stir well, test for seasoning and correct if necessary. Pour into a heated serving dish and serve immediately.

Chapter Ten

SWEET DISHES, SPECIAL FRUIT TARTS AND TRADITIONAL CAKES

Sweet Dishes

In the French repertory, sweet dishes are more than just sweet. They all have an additional, subtle flavour, even the simple homely ones served to point the fact that Sunday is a day of leisure on the farm. This subtlety may be imparted by rum, brandy, fruit liqueur or just vanilla. But if vanilla is used it is in the pod, which gives a much finer, more natural flavour than vanilla essence. The pod may be used up to five times if, after the first three times, it is split down the length.

Crème de semoule aux abricots
(Apricot and Semolina Mould)
Serves 6

175 g (6 oz) large dried apricots
juice 1 large orange
4½ tablespoons sugar
200 ml (7 fl oz) water
2 medium sized eggs
900 ml (1½ pints) full-cream milk
1 vanilla pod
3 tablespoons semolina
1 tablespoon chopped candied orange peel
4 tablespoons apricot liqueur
a 1 litre (2 pint) charlotte mould

Soak the apricots overnight in the strained orange juice with 2 teaspoons sugar.

Add the water to the fruit and juice and pour into a small pan. Cover and bring to boiling point slowly over low heat. Simmer until tender and leave to cool.

Separate the eggs. Heat the milk and vanilla pod in a large saucepan over low heat, add the remaining sugar and stir until dissolved. When a white froth starts to rise sprinkle in the semolina, stir well and cook, stirring constantly with a wooden spatula until the mixture thickens and leaves the bottom of the pan clean when the spatula is drawn across it. This will take about 10 minutes. Draw the pan from the heat, remove the vanilla pod and wash and dry it for future use. Stir in the egg yolks and leave to cool, covered with a buttered paper pressed on to the surface to prevent a skin forming.

Heat the oven to 180°C, 350°F, Gas 4.

Drain the apricots and reserve the juice. Cut the apricots into halves. Line the base of the charlotte mould with apricots placed cut side uppermost and closely together. Cut any that are left over into small pieces and add the chopped candied orange peel. Stir this fruit into the semolina mixture.

Beat the egg whites to a stiff peak and fold them into the contents of the pan a third at a time, taking care not to beat or stir them in. Pour the mixture into the mould, stand it in a baking tin half full of hot water and cook in the centre of the oven for 30 to 35 minutes until the centre is firm to the touch. Leave to cool in the oven with the door slightly open. When cold, refrigerate until required.

To serve, pass a thin-bladed knife around the sides of the mould, place a serving dish on top, invert quickly and set down with a sharp tap to unmould. Mix the liqueur with the reserved fruit juices and pour over the top.

Charlotte aux pommes
(Apple Charlotte with White Wine)
Serves 4–6

1 kg (2 lb) dessert apples (Cox's or Golden
  Delicious)
juice 1 lemon
60 g (2½ oz) unsalted butter
150 ml (¼ pint) white wine (sweet or dry)
2 tablespoons sugar
1 vanilla pod
1 stale white loaf (450 g [1 lb])
a 1 litre (2 pint) charlotte mould

Peel the apples and drop them into a bowl of
cold water to which the lemon juice has been
added, to prevent discolouration. Melt 50 g
(2 oz) butter in a *sauteuse* or very large frying
pan over low heat, add the wine, sugar and
vanilla pod and bring very slowly to boiling
point. Meanwhile, cut the apples into thick
slices working around the core and dropping
the slices immediately into the pan. Arrange
in one layer, if possible, cover and cook very
gently until tender. They must remain whole.
Remove with a slotted spoon and set aside,
reserving the juices in the pan. Remove the
vanilla pod, wash and dry it for future use.

Heat the oven to 200°C, 400°F, Gas 6. Coat
the mould thickly with the remaining butter.

Cut one slice of bread 3 mm (⅛ inch) thick,
remove the crust and shape it to fit the bottom
of the mould; cut another to fit the top. Slice
the rest of the bread and then cut into fingers
about 4 cm (1½ inches) wide and long
enough to stand up 2.5 cm (1 inch) over the
rim of the mould. Dip each one lightly into
the pan juices on one side only and line the
mould with the slices placed dipped side out-
wards and slightly overlapping each other.
Fill with apple, place the second circle of
dipped bread on top, fold over the side pieces
to cover and press down firmly with the palm.
Place in the centre of the oven and bake for
about 1 hour.

The *charlotte* must be well-crusted and gold-
en brown all over when served. To test, pass a
knife down the side of the mould, carefully
press it inwards in order to see the sides and if
not crusted and brown cover the top with a
lightly balanced piece of foil to prevent burning and cook for a further 15 to 20 minutes at
slightly increased heat. Remove from the oven
and allow to settle for a few moments before
unmoulding.

To serve, pass a thin-bladed knife around
the sides of the mould, place a heated serving
dish on top, invert quickly and set down with
a sharp tap to unmould. Serve immediately
with thick cream.

All over France the popular *clafoutis* is
made in early summer when black cherries are in season. In the Auvergne the
added flavouring of Armagnac puts it into
a class of its own. Cherry brandy may be
used as an alternative.

Clafoutis auvergnat
(Auvergne Clafoutis with Brandy)
Serves 6

450 g (1 lb) firm black cherries
200 g (7 oz) flour
3 medium sized eggs
salt
about 400 ml (¾ pint) milk
4 tablespoons Armagnac or cherry brandy
60 g (2½ oz) castor sugar
40 g (1½ oz) butter
a shallow baking dish or cake tin, 19 cm
  (7½ inches) diameter × 5 cm (2 inches)
deep

Heat the oven to 200°C, 400°F, Gas 6.
Remove the stalks from the cherries, wash and
leave to drain.

Sift the flour into a mixing bowl and make

a well in the centre. Separate the eggs and mix the yolks with a pinch of salt and a little of the milk. Pour them into the flour and beat with a wire whisk, gradually adding more milk until a batter the consistency of thick double cream is obtained. Add the Armagnac or cherry brandy, stir well and set aside. The batter can be made in advance and the liqueur added just before it is cooked.

Beat the egg whites, adding the sugar little by little, until a stiff glossy peak forms. Dry the cherries and fold the beaten whites and cherries into the batter a third at a time. To fold them in, place a third on top of the batter and with a wooden spatula dip down into the mixture, along the bottom of the bowl, up and over the whites with a twist of the spatula so that the batter surrounds them. In this way the whites will be incorporated without losing the air beaten into them.

Butter the oven dish, pour in the mixture, scatter small flecks of butter over the surface and bake for 15 to 20 minutes or until well risen and the centre is just firm when pressed with a fingertip.

Sprinkle with more castor sugar and serve immediately.

It is not traditional to serve the usual *clafoutis* with cream, but as this one is special the exception can be made.

Crème frite aux noisettes
(Hazelnut Cream Fritters)
Serves 4–6

100 g (4 oz) hazelnuts
5 medium sized eggs
225 g (8 oz) sugar
200 g (7 oz) flour
3 medium sized egg yolks
750 ml (1¼ pints) milk
1 vanilla pod
3 tablespoons rum

225 g (8 oz) stale white bread
salt
oil for deep frying
castor sugar

Place the hazelnuts under a medium grill and heat until the skin rubs off easily between the fingers. Chop finely and set aside.

Break 3 whole eggs into a bowl, add the sugar and beat until it dissolves. Gradually sift in the flour, beating it in and adding the extra yolks at the same time. Boil the milk with the vanilla pod. Remove the pod and beat the milk slowly into the egg mixture. Wash and dry the pod for future use. Pour the mixture back into the pan, place over gentle heat and stir until the first bubbles rise. Allow the bubbles to increase for 1 minute, no longer. Remove the pan from the heat and stir in the rum and chopped hazelnuts. Allow to cool for a few minutes, then pour on to an oiled slab and shape with an oiled knife into a large rectangle about 2 cm (¾ inch) thick. Leave to set for several hours, overnight if possible. Again using an oiled knife, cut into bands 5 cm (2 inches) wide and cut these diagonally into diamond shapes.

Grate the stale bread into fine crumbs. Beat the remaining eggs with a pinch of salt in a large soup-plate, dip the prepared pieces of *crème* first into the beaten egg, then into breadcrumbs, and place in a wire frying basket. Heat the oil until smoking and lower the basket into the oil. The little fritters must colour to the golden stage very quickly so that they do not melt inside.

Drain, sprinkle with castor sugar and serve immediately.

Flan aux raisins
(Grape Flan)
Serves 6

225 g (8 oz) frozen puff pastry
450 g (1 lb) large green grapes
225 g (8 oz) large black grapes
2 medium sized eggs
100 g (4 oz) castor sugar
3 tablespoons ground almonds
100 ml (4 fl oz) double cream
a 25 cm (10 inch) flan tin with loose base

Thaw the pastry at room temperature for 1 hour.

Butter and flour the flan tin. Roll the pastry out and line the tin. Heat the oven to 230°C, 450°F, Gas 8, with a baking sheet on the middle shelf.

Wash and drain the grapes and remove them from the stalks. Pat with kitchen paper until completely dry. Arrange them closely in the pastry case. Beat the eggs and sugar together until thick and foaming, then beat in the ground almonds and finally the cream. Spread evenly over the grapes and bake in the centre of the oven for 20 minutes. Reduce the heat to 200°C, 400°F, Gas 6 and bake for a further 20 minutes.

If the surface browns too quickly balance a sheet of foil lightly on top until the flan is cooked.

Carefully lift up the pastry with a spatula to make sure the bottom crust is firm and cooked and bake for a further 10 minutes if necessary.

Cool for 5 minutes, remove the outer rim of the flan tin and serve warm.

When strawberries are scarce French country women serve the fruit in this delectable way.

Fraises à la crème
(Strawberries, Liqueur and Cream)
Serves 4–5

450 g (1 lb) strawberries
4 tablespoons castor sugar
4 tablespoons curaçao or cherry brandy
300 ml ($\frac{1}{2}$ pint) double cream
2 dry macaroons

Wash and dry the strawberries quickly and remove the stalks. Place them in a wide serving bowl and sprinkle with the castor sugar. Cover and leave in a cool place (but not refrigerated) for 1 hour. Pour the liqueur over them, cover, and leave for a further 2 hours or until required.

When ready to serve, if the cream is liquid whisk it until fairly thick, sweeten to taste with more castor sugar and crumble in the macaroons. Pour this mixture over the fruit and mix it all carefully with two forks so that the strawberries are not crushed. Serve immediately.

Fraises à l'orange
(Strawberries with Orange)
Serves 6

4 oranges
4 tablespoons castor sugar
450 g (1 lb) strawberries
juice $\frac{1}{2}$ lemon

Grate the rind of 2 oranges and set aside. Peel all 4 oranges, cutting off the peel and pith in one operation with a sharp knife. Slice the fruit thinly and remove the pips. (Do this over a large plate in order to reserve the juice.) Place the orange slices and their juice in a wide bowl and sprinkle half the sugar over them.

Wash and dry the strawberries quickly and remove the stalks. Cut the biggest ones into halves and arrange them all in one layer over the oranges. Mix the grated orange rind into the rest of the sugar and sprinkle this over the strawberries. Cover and leave in a cool place but not refrigerated for at least 2 hours. Refrigerate 30 minutes before serving. When ready to serve, strain the lemon juice over the fruit and carefully turn it over and over with a wooden fork and spoon as when turning a salad.

Curd cheese is made in most French farmhouses from skimmed milk and is used a great deal in cooking. It can be bought in bulk from our own delicatessen shops, and it is essential for the success of these recipes to use this type of curd cheese and not the processed variety sold in cartons.

Gâteau au fromage blanc
(Hot Cheesecake)
Serves 6

3 large eggs
350 g (12 oz) curd cheese
salt
5 tablespoons castor sugar
grated rind 1 lemon
4 tablespoons flour
grated rind 1 orange
2 tablespoons finely chopped candied orange and lemon peel
a cake tin, 15 cm (6 inches) diameter × 5 cm (2 inches) deep

Preheat the oven to 190°C, 375°F, Gas 5.

Separate the eggs, putting the yolks into one bowl and 2 of the whites into another. Empty the curd cheese into a mixing bowl. Beat a pinch of salt into the egg yolks and stir them into the cheese. When thoroughly blended, stir in the sugar until dissolved and then add the grated lemon rind. Sieve the flour into this mixture, beat until quite smooth, stir in the grated orange rind and the candied peel.

Beat the egg whites to a stiff peak and *fold* them into the cheese mixture a third at a time. Butter the cake tin, sprinkle evenly with flour, and pour in the mixture to three quarters full. Bake for 30 minutes without opening the oven door. Increase the heat to 200°C, 400°F, Gas 6 and cook for 1 hour further or until the centre is set and a pointed knife plunged into it comes out clean. If the surface colours too much during this time, cover with a sheet of foil. Remove from the oven and leave for 5 minutes before unmoulding.

To serve, pass a thin-bladed knife round the inside of the tin, place a heated serving plate on top and, holding them together with both hands, invert, setting the plate down with a sharp tap to unmould. Sprinkle with castor sugar and serve warm with thick cream.

Alternatively, serve with curd cheese beaten to a thick cream consistency with a little milk and sugar. In French farmhouses, this is frequently served with sweet dishes or soft fruit, instead of cream.

Niort, the chief town of Deux-Sèvres, is known for its production of candied angelica, its dungeons, its leather trade and because it was the birthplace of Madame de Maintenon. Schoolchildren and gourmets take these facts in this order, since angelica is used to flavour many sweet dishes of the region.

Gâteau de riz à l'angélique
(Rice and Angelica Mould)
Serves 4–6

100 g (4 oz) long-grain rice
40 g (1½ oz) angelica
3 medium sized eggs
350 ml (12 fl oz) milk
1 vanilla pod
salt
30 g (1¼ oz) butter
about 90 g (3½ oz) sugar
2 tablespoons *chapelure* (see page 67)
a 1 litre (2 pint) charlotte mould

Wash the rice under cold running water until the water is no longer cloudy, drain and scatter into a panful of fast-boiling water. Boil for 2 minutes exactly. Drain and wash under tepid water, and leave in the sieve. Chop the angelica. Separate the eggs and beat the yolks.

Pour half the milk into a large saucepan, add the vanilla pod, a pinch of salt and 20 g (¾ oz) butter and bring slowly to boiling point over medium low heat. Scatter in the rice and stir with a wooden spoon. Reduce the heat to low, cover and cook slowly until the milk is absorbed. Meanwhile heat the rest of the milk to boiling point and add it half at a time to the rice, cooking the rice in the same way, covered, until all the milk is absorbed. Stir occasionally with a fork to separate the grains.

When the mixture is creamy and the rice soft, remove the vanilla pod and wash and dry it for future use. Sweeten the rice to taste with about 60 g (2½ oz) sugar and when the sugar has dissolved, stir in the chopped angelica and beaten egg yolks. Leave until cold.

Heat the oven to 180°C, 350°F, Gas 4.

Thickly coat the charlotte mould with the remaining butter. Mix 2 tablespoons sugar with the *chapelure* and sprinkle round the inside of the mould. Beat the egg whites to a stiff peak and fold into the rice, a third at a time, with a wooden spatula. Do not beat or stir. Pour the mixture into the prepared mould. Bake in the centre of the oven for 40 minutes until brown on top. Turn off the heat, open the oven door and leave the *gâteau* inside for 10 minutes to settle.

To serve, pass a thin-bladed knife round the inside of the mould, place a warm serving plate on top and holding them both together, invert quickly and set the plate down with a sharp tap to unmould.

Serve warm with thick cream.

There is no equivalent to the word pudding in the French language. The French regard this type of sweet dish as superfluous for everyday meals when cheese and fruit are much more to their taste as wine-drinkers.

However, the word *pouding* has gradually crept into their language to describe sweet dishes imagined to be English. Native sweet dishes are also known as *gâteaux* when they are cooked in a mould.

One such dish which could be called *pouding* was popular in Napoleon's time perhaps because the recipe was brought to France by his consort, Joséphine de Beauharnais, from Martinique—or so legend has it.

Gâteau de Sainte Luce
(Banana Pudding with Raspberry Sauce)
Serves 6

2 large new-laid eggs
300 ml ($\frac{1}{2}$ pint) fresh milk
4 large ripe bananas
7 tablespoons stale breadcrumbs
about 5 tablespoons sugar
grated rind and juice 1 lemon
juice $\frac{1}{2}$ orange
4 tablespoons dark rum
100 g (4 oz) unsalted butter
sauce à la framboise (see following recipe)

Both the eggs and the milk should be as fresh as possible to avoid curdling.

Using a large mixing bowl, mash the bananas smooth with a fork and beat in the eggs, breadcrumbs and 4 tablespoons sugar. Add the grated lemon rind, strained lemon and orange juices and the rum. Melt the butter and, reserving 1 teaspoonful, beat the remainder into the milk, then beat into the banana mixture.

Butter a large pudding basin with the reserved butter, coat with sugar and pour in the

banana mixture. Cover with buttered grease-proof paper and a sheet of foil, pleated in the centre to allow for rising. Tie down with string and place in a large pan half filled with simmering water. Cover and steam over low heat for $1\frac{1}{4}$ to $1\frac{1}{2}$ hours, keeping the level of the water maintained by adding a little more when necessary. This water must never boil fast.

To serve, remove the foil and paper from the pudding, pass a palette knife dipped in boiling water round the inside of the basin, put a heated serving dish on top and holding them both together with an ovencloth, quickly invert and set the dish down with a sharp tap to unmould. Pour the *sauce à la framboise* over and serve immediately.

Sauce à la framboise
(Raspberry Sauce)

225 g (8 oz) raspberries (fresh or frozen)
2 tablespoons castor sugar
juice 1 lemon

Place the raspberries in a wide bowl, sprinkle with sugar, cover, and leave at room temperature to render their juice. After 1 hour bruise the fruit lightly with the bottom of a bottle, add the strained lemon juice, mix carefully with a wooden spoon and leave until required.

Mousse glacée au rhum
(Iced Rum Mousse)
Serves 6–8

4 large eggs
150 g (5 oz) castor sugar
4 tablespoons dark rum
300 ml (½ pint) double cream

Separate the eggs. Place a very large pan half full of hot water over medium-low heat so that the water will remain very hot without boiling. Put the egg yolks into a slightly smaller pan that will stand in the first one but still be large enough to accommodate a considerable quantity of beaten egg whites. Add the sugar and the rum and, stirring constantly with a wooden spatula, heat the mixture until it forms a thick ribbon when dropped from the spatula. Remove the pan from the water and continue stirring until the mixture is cold.

Beat the cream until thick and beat the egg whites to a stiff peak. Fold the cream into the egg yolk mixture, then fold in the whites a third at a time with a wooden spatula, taking care not to stir them in. Pour into a metal mould, place in the freezing compartment of the refrigerator and freeze for 8 hours.

Do not remove from the freezing compartment until required to serve. Divide between the necessary number of chilled long-stemmed glasses and serve with boudoir biscuits.

Pain perdu
(Baked Apricot Crisps)
Serves 4

8 slices stale bread (2 cm [¾ inch] thick)
2 medium sized eggs
300 ml (½ pint) milk
½ sachet vanilla sugar (10 g [⅓ oz])
salt
7 g (¼ oz) butter
4 ripe apricots
castor sugar

Heat the oven to 200°C, 400°F, Gas 6.

Using a pastry cutter, stamp out circles from the bread, 4 cm (1½ inches) in diameter. Mix the eggs, milk, vanilla sugar and a pinch of salt together in a soup-plate. Coat a Swiss roll tin with the butter. Slit the apricots round down the crease, then twist the two halves in opposite directions to separate and remove the stone. Dip each circle of bread in the egg and milk mixture, put half an apricot on each one, cut side uppermost, and sprinkle liberally with castor sugar. Place them on the buttered tin and bake for about 15 minutes or until crisp and brown and the fruit is melting.

Serve very hot.

Large ripe plums can be used for this recipe in place of apricots.

When dark purple plums come into season, this is the time to make the best of all plum tarts known on the farms of western France as *le pruné*.

Le pruné
(Farmhouse Plum Tart)
Serves 4

Pâte sablée
salt
175 g (6 oz) plain flour
75 g (3 oz) slightly salted butter
2 tablespoons granulated sugar
1 medium sized egg
1 tablespoon cold water
a 20 cm (8 inch) flan tin with loose base

Filling
450 g (1 lb) dark purple plums
3–4 tablespoons castor sugar

Add a pinch of salt to the flour and sift it into a bowl. Rub in the butter with the fingertips and when the consistency of fine breadcrumbs is obtained add the sugar and mix well. Beat the egg with the water and bind the pastry with it. Work in all the crumbs and form into a ball. Wrap in foil and chill until required.

To make the filling, wash the plums, slit them round through the crease and twist in opposite directions to separate into halves. Place in one layer in a large pan cut side down, cover and set over low heat. Do not add water. When the fruit is boiling, remove the lid and simmer until reduced to purée and very little juice remains. Remove the stones and leave to cool. When cold, add sugar to taste.

Butter and flour the flan tin. Heat the oven to 190° C, 375° F, Gas 5, with a baking sheet inside. Flatten the ball of pastry on a board with a few strokes of the rolling pin, transfer to the tin and work it evenly round the tin with the thumbs. This pastry is crumbly to handle but when it breaks just press it together again or add pieces by pressing them in. Trim the edge and roll the trimmings into 2 long bands. Cut each one into 3 narrow strips and set aside. Scatter a thin layer of sugar over the base of the pastry case. Fill evenly with plum purée. Taking up the bands of pastry with both hands, twist them in opposite directions. Lay them across the fruit like the spokes of a wheel and press the ends down on to the pastry rim.

Bake for 25 minutes, increase the heat to 200° C, 400° F, Gas 6, and cook for a further 10 minutes. If the tart is browning too fast lightly balance a piece of foil on top when the heat is increased. Cool on a wire rack, remove the outer rim of the flan tin and serve warm with thick cream.

The canned morello cherries used in this recipe can be obtained in this country from specialist grocers, but sweet red dessert cherries may be used if preferred.

Riz à l'empereur
(Creamed Rice with Cherries)
Serves 4–6

450 g (1 lb) canned morello cherries
4 tablespoons cherry brandy or kirsch
100 g (4 oz) long-grain rice
350 ml (12 fl oz) full-cream milk
1 vanilla pod
3–4 tablespoons granulated sugar
2 tablespoons castor sugar ·
300 ml ($\frac{1}{2}$ pint) cream

Drain the cherries and place the fruit in a flat dish. Pour the liqueur over them and leave to macerate until required.

Cook the rice as advised in *gâteau de riz à l'angélique* (page 152), adding the milk a little at a time until the mixture is creamy and the rice cooked. Remove the vanilla pod and wash and dry it for future use.

Sweeten the rice to taste with sugar remembering that sweetened cream will be added to it later. Leave to cool completely. Pick out 10 or 12 cherries for decoration and set aside. Beat the castor sugar into the cream and when thick pour into a large decorative bowl, add the creamed rice, the cherries and liqueur and mix carefully with two forks.

Arrange the reserved cherries on top and chill until required.

The weekday farm meals usually end in winter with an orange, an apple or a pear. On Sundays this is turned into something more exciting at little cost. In their simple way these fruit dishes are very good indeed and quite enough to end a large French lunch, more as a full stop than an entire sentence.

Oranges à la basquaise
(Hot Orange Slices)
Serves 4

4 oranges
4–5 tablespoons castor sugar
2 medium sized eggs
1 tablespoon corn oil
50 g (2 oz) unsalted butter

For each person choose a ripe medium sized orange with a smooth skin. Wash and dry them and remove a slice from top and bottom. Cut them into fine slices 3 mm ($\frac{1}{8}$ inch) thick, peel included, and remove the pips with a pointed knife. If the slices are large cut them into halves. Sprinkle liberally with sugar on both sides and press it into the fruit. Beat the eggs and oil together in a large shallow dish and soak the orange slices in the mixture, turning them over frequently. Melt the butter in a large frying pan over low heat and when foaming place the slices in it, one layer at a time. When coloured golden brown on one side, turn them over and colour the other side. As they are browned, remove from the pan with a slotted spoon and keep hot on a serving plate in the oven. If the butter turns dark before all the slices are cooked, empty the pan, wipe it clean with paper and melt fresh butter to cook the rest.

To serve, place a cocktail stick in each slice, sprinkle with more castor sugar and serve hot.

Pommes au beurre
(Caramel Apple Slices)
Serves 4

juice 1 lemon
750 g (1$\frac{1}{2}$ lb) large dessert apples (preferably Cox's)
50 g (2 oz) unsalted butter
castor sugar

Pour the lemon juice into a soup-plate. Peel and core the apples, cut into rings 1 cm ($\frac{1}{2}$ inch) thick and turn them in lemon juice as soon as they are cut.

Melt the butter over low heat in a large frying pan and when foaming turn the apple slices in it to coat on both sides. Arrange in one layer on the bottom of the pan, increase the heat slightly and cook until golden underneath. When cooking a large quantity, if the butter turns dark before all the fruit is cooked pour it away, wipe out the pan and melt fresh butter. Heat the grill at maximum temperature.

When cooked on one side transfer the apple rings to a flameproof plate, uncooked side uppermost, and place under the grill about 10 cm (4 inches) from the element. Grill for 2 minutes, sprinkle thickly with sugar and grill until the sugar bubbles and then turns golden brown. Allow to cool for a minute so that the sugar hardens and crisps, and serve warm.

If the apples are very sweet and ripe they make a satisfying last touch to a rich meal when sprinkled lightly with salt instead of sugar.

Poires grillées au miel
(Pears Grilled with Honey)
Serves 4

4 large ripe William pears
juice 1 lemon
25 g (1 oz) unsalted butter
100 ml (4 fl oz) double cream
about 1 tablespoon honey
about 1 tablespoon sugar

Wash and dry the pears. Cut in half lengthways and hollow out the core with a teaspoon, making a cavity. Rub the cut surface with lemon juice and pour 1 teaspoon lemon juice into each hollow. Melt the butter and brush the cut surface with it. Arrange the pears head to tail and cut side down in a flameproof dish, pour the rest of the lemon juice into the dish and set aside until 30 minutes before serving. Whip the cream until firm and chill until required.

Heat the grill to maximum.

Place the pears under the grill about 10 cm (4 inches) from the element. Grill for 10 minutes. Turn them over, brush with butter again, fill the hollow with honey and trail a thread of honey over the cut surface, sprinkle thickly with sugar and replace under the grill for about 15 minutes until brown on top.

Allow to cool for a few moments, place a spoonful of cream on each pear and serve warm with the juices from the dish poured over the cream.

The French country way of making fruit ice-cream is simple to a degree and cannot be bettered for both flavour and consistency. Any soft fruit can be used and a mixture is even better. The best combination is raspberries and loganberries.

Crème glacée aux fruits
(Iced Fruit Cream)
Serves 4

300 ml ($\frac{1}{2}$ pint) thick Jersey or Devonshire cream
225 g (8 oz) ripe soft fruit
75 g (3 oz) castor sugar
a 450 g (1 lb) loaf tin

If the cream used is the ordinary double variety, beat it lightly with a whisk until thick and chill until required.

Pick over the fruit and place in a warm mixing bowl. Put it into a warm oven for 20 minutes to make the juice flow. Crush with the bottom of a bottle. Work the fruit through a fine sieve with a wooden spoon to obtain a thick, seedless purée. Stir in the sugar until dissolved, then add the cream and stir until incorporated. Pour into the loaf tin, cover with foil, and freeze until firm.

Special Fruit Tarts

The tart for special occasions (*la tarte de cérémonie*) is made at home by farming people. They prefer their own family recipes for these events to the excellent but less exciting fruit tarts made by the *pâtissier* of their neighbouring village.

In the following tart, the sharp flavour of morello cherries contrasts deliciously with the sweet almond filling. If morellos are unobtainable red dessert cherries can be used, but they should not be too sweet.

Tarte frangipane aux cerises
(Almond and Cherry Tart)
Serves 6

Pâte sucrée
225 g (8 oz) flour
salt
100 g (4 oz) butter
75 g (3 oz) sugar
1 medium sized egg
a 25 cm (10 inch) flan tin with loose base

Filling
450 g (1 lb) morello cherries (fresh or canned)
125 g (4 oz) unsalted butter
125 g (4 oz) sugar
125 g (4 oz) ground almonds
1 teaspoon flour
2 large eggs
2 tablespoons rum

Glazing
175 g (6 oz) icing sugar
1 tablespoon rum
2 tablespoons water
redcurrant jelly

Sift the flour with a pinch of salt and set aside on a folded paper. Drop the butter into a warm mixing bowl, add the sugar, and work with a wooden spatula until soft and creamy. Add the egg and work together until smooth. Pour in the flour all at once, beating constantly, then work lightly with the hand until a soft ball is formed and the bowl is clean. Place the ball on the pastry board and push it forward and down with the heel of the hand gathering it up with the fingers before repeating the movement. Do this 3 or 4 times. This *foulage* incorporates the ingredients and makes the pastry smooth. Cut the ball into quarters, place one on top of the other and push down with the palm. Roll out a little, cut again and repeat this operation twice. Chill for 1 hour.

Butter the flan tin. Roll out the pastry to 5 mm ($\frac{1}{4}$ inch) in thickness. Line the tin, and if the pastry breaks, seal it together with the fingertips. Trim the edges and prick the base with a fork. Chill for 30 minutes.

Heat the oven to 200°C, 400°F, Gas 6, with a baking sheet on the middle shelf.

To make the filling, wash and dry the cherries if fresh and remove the stones, or drain if canned. Drop the butter into a warmed bowl and work to a cream with a wooden spoon, add the sugar, ground almonds and flour, and beat with a hand whisk to a smooth cream. Add the eggs one at a time, beat them in thoroughly, stir in rum. Arrange the cherries in the bottom of the pastry case, pour the cream evenly over them.

Bake for about 30 minutes or until the surface is coloured to the golden stage, then cover lightly with a sheet of foil and continue cooking. Count 1 hour 10 minutes' baking time in all. Remove from the oven and place on a wire tray to cool.

Meanwhile, put the icing sugar, rum and water into a small pan and dissolve the sugar over low heat, beating constantly. Heat some redcurrant jelly to a spreading consistency. Brush the surface of the tart with redcurrant jelly, pour the glaze over it and smooth evenly with a metal spatula.

Serve either warm or cold.

Gâteau des rois (see page 164).

158

Anjou is famous for its good food, its fine white wines and its fruit—peaches and pears especially. William pears are used to make a farmhouse tart for which the area is noted.

Tarte aux poires à l'angevine
(Anjou Pear Tart)
Serves 6–8

Pâte sucrée
225 g (8 oz) flour
salt
100 g (4 oz) butter
75 g (3 oz) sugar
1 medium sized egg yolk
2 tablespoons water
a 25 cm (10 inch) flan tin with loose base

Filling
5 large William pears
40 g (1½ oz) unsalted butter
75 g (3 oz) sugar
1 sachet vanilla sugar (20 g [⅔ oz])
6 tablespoons double cream

Sift the flour with a pinch of salt into a bowl and add the butter cut into small pieces. Rub it in with the fingertips until finely crumbled and stir in the sugar. Beat the egg yolk with the water and pour it into the centre of the flour mixture. Gather in the flour with the fingers, working round the bowl, and quickly form the pastry into a ball. Chill for 30 minutes.

Heat the oven to 200°C, 400°F, Gas 6, with a baking sheet on the middle shelf.

Butter and flour the tin. Roll out the pastry and line the tin, prick the bottom with a fork and line with greaseproof paper. Fill with dried beans or little pebbles and bake for 20 to 25 minutes. Remove the beans and paper and leave to cool on a wire tray. When cold, remove the outer rim of the tin.

Meanwhile prepare the filling. Peel the pears and cut each one into 8 sections, over a plate to recover the juices. Remove the core. Melt the butter in a *sauteuse* or large frying pan and when foaming sauté the pears over gentle heat, shaking the pan to prevent sticking. Sprinkle with 25 g (1 oz) sugar and all of the vanilla sugar. Turn the pears over and as soon as they become transparent and tender, lift them out with a slotted spoon and drain over the pan to recover the syrup. Set aside until required.

Heat the grill to maximum.

Pour the cream and reserved juices into the pan, mix them thoroughly with the syrup and stirring constantly reduce the mixture over medium-high heat until it thickens. Remove the pan from the heat, arrange the fruit in the pastry case, and pour the cream mixture over it. Sprinkle with the remaining sugar and place under the grill to colour lightly. Take care that it does not burn.

Allow to cool for a few minutes and serve warm.

Le macaroné (see page 165), *oranges à la basquaise* (see page 156), *poires grillées au miel* (see page 157).

Tarte soufflée aux abricots
(Soufflé Apricot Tart)
Serves 6

pâte sucrée (see page 161)
a 25 cm (10 inch) flan tin with loose base

Filling
5 medium sized eggs
175 g (6 oz) sugar
50 g (2 oz) flour
500 ml (18 fl oz) milk
1 vanilla pod
salt
12 apricot halves, fresh or tinned
2–3 tablespoons apricot jam
icing sugar

Make the pastry. Butter the flan tin and line with pastry. Chill for 30 minutes.

Separate the eggs. Beat the egg yolks with the sugar in a large bowl until dissolved. Add the flour and beat well together. Heat the milk with the vanilla pod and, when boiling, remove the pod and pour the milk on to the egg mixture, beating vigorously meanwhile with a wire whisk. Leave to cool. Wash and dry the vanilla pod for future use. Heat the oven to 200°C, 400°F, Gas 6, with a baking sheet on the middle shelf.

Beat the egg whites to a stiff peak with a pinch of salt and *fold* them into the cold mixture with an up-and-over movement so that they are incorporated without being beaten or stirred.

With a large icing nozzle, pipe the mixture on to the pastry to cover evenly. Make small hollows on the surface and place a half apricot on each, cut side uppermost. Bake on the heated baking sheet for 40 minutes, watching carefully that the surface of the tart does not brown too deeply. Leave to cool. When cold, remove rim from tin.

To serve, melt the jam until just liquid, dust the tart liberally with icing sugar and glaze the fruit with jam lightly brushed over it.

Traditional Cakes

Although the French have no Christmas pudding, they have a *bûche flambante*, a light dessert cake soaked in rum and served surrounded by shimmering blue flames, which makes an excellent and most decorative alternative.

Bûche flambante
(Yule Log, Flambé)
Serves 8

225 g (8 oz) Allinsons plain Farmhouse flour (81%) (obtainable at health food shops)
10 g ($\frac{1}{3}$ oz) bakers' yeast
5 tablespoons warm milk (hand-hot)
1 teaspoon sugar
salt
2 medium sized eggs
75 g (3 oz) butter
a long cake tin, 23 × 10 × 6 cm (9 × 4 × 2$\frac{1}{2}$ inches)

Rum syrup
300 g (10 oz) sugar
500 ml (18 fl oz) water
150 ml ($\frac{1}{4}$ pint) rum

Glazing and decoration
225 g (8 oz) apricot jam
glacé cherries
angelica
1 orange
150 ml ($\frac{1}{4}$ pint) rum

It is essential to use the flour specified, because it is the nearest to the French *farine de gruau*.

Sift the flour into the warmed bowl of an electric blender and make a hollow in the centre. Crumble the yeast into the warm milk and beat until dissolved. Pour into the flour and mix with a wooden spatula until it is incorporated. Sprinkle the sugar and salt over the dough, mix again, add the eggs and work until smooth. Then blend with the dough-hook attachment, on mark 3 for about 3 minutes. Increase to 5 and beat for about 7 minutes. Stop the machine and scrape the dough off the hook when it forms a ball. Beat for 10 to 15 minutes in all. Cover with a cloth and leave in a warm place for 1 hour. The dough will double in volume.

Soften the butter in a warm bowl until creamy. Work it into the dough a third at a time with the spatula. Blend on mark 1 for 2 minutes. The success of the cake depends on thorough beating. Heat the oven to 140°C, 275°F, Gas 1.

Warm the tin, butter it lightly, pour in the mixture to half fill, smooth down evenly and leave on the middle shelf of the oven until the dough fills the tin (about 20 minutes). Increase the heat to 220°C, 425°F, Gas 7, and bake for 15 minutes. Reduce the heat to 200°C, 400°F, Gas 6, and continue baking for a further 15 minutes. When cooked, a knitting needle plunged into the centre will come out clean. Leave the cake in the tin on a wire rack to cool.

Meanwhile, make the rum syrup. Dissolve the sugar in the water and rum over medium heat, stirring frequently, and leave slowly simmering.

Unmould the cake, place on the rack upside down and, with a very sharp knife, trim off the square edges down the length to obtain a rough log-shape. Place the rack over a large meat plate, bring the syrup to the fast boiling point and *very slowly* pour it over the entire surface of the cake. Remove the rack, pour the syrup back into the pan, replace the rack, re-boil the syrup and pour over the cake again. Repeat until the syrup is all absorbed. The cake will increase considerably in volume. Allow to cool before glazing and decorating.

Place both hands along the sides of the cake and carefully transfer it to a serving dish.

To make the glaze, melt the jam until warm and liquidise in a blender to obtain a thick purée or rub through a sieve with a wooden spoon. Glaze the entire surface with apricot purée to retain the moisture, smoothing it

evenly with a metal spatula, and decorate with whole and halved cherries, leaves of angelica and thin slices of orange cut into halves.

To serve the cake *flambé*, heat the rum in a small jug placed in a saucepan of very hot water over low heat. When the rum is hot, place the cake on the table, pour the rum around it, ignite and baste until the flames die down. Serve cut into thick slices with a little of the rum poured over each one.

Twelfth Night is still celebrated in most French country households by inviting friends, after dinner, to share a bottle of dessert wine and a *gâteau des rois*. This special cake is cut into the same number of pieces as there are guests and the one who finds in his or her share a tiny porcelain doll is proclaimed king or queen. They must then choose a consort and invite all present to share the same ceremony at a future date.

This custom, relic of a pagan feast, is anticipated with pleasure in the country where it affords many pleasant evenings. In Anjou the cake is an especially good one, but then this is a region especially known for its excellent food and wines. A dried bean, though less romantic, can be substituted for the porcelain doll.

Gâteau des rois
(Twelfth Night Cake)
Serves 6–8

400 g (14 oz) frozen puff pastry
1 small egg yolk
1 tablespoon milk

Filling
150 g (5 oz) ground almonds
100 g (4 oz) sugar
2 medium sized eggs

Glazing
50 g (2 oz) ground almonds
50 g (2 oz) sugar
1 egg white
icing sugar

Remove the pastry from the freezer 1 hour before required.

Divide the pastry in two parts, one fractionally bigger than the other. Roll out to a thickness of 5 mm ($\frac{1}{4}$ inch). Using two dinner plates, one slightly larger than the other, cut out one circle 23 cm (9 inches) in diameter and the other 24 cm (9$\frac{1}{2}$ inches) in diameter. Slide the larger circle on to a floured paper.

Heat the oven to 200°C, 400°F, Gas 6, with a baking sheet on the middle shelf.

To make the filling, mix the ground almonds, sugar and eggs to a thick smooth paste and set aside.

Beat the egg yolk with the milk and brush it round the edge of the larger circle in a 1 cm ($\frac{1}{2}$ inch) wide band. Heap the almond filling in the centre, place the smaller piece of pastry on top and fold the brushed edge over on to it, sealing the two together. Press down this edge with the side of the hand. Cover a round bread board with foil, hold it closely over the cake with both hands, gather up the floured paper against it and invert quickly to turn the cake on to the foil, the larger circle now on top. Press down the outer edge again.

To make the glaze, mix the ground almonds with the sugar and unbeaten egg white and spread it all over the cake with a metal spatula. Sprinkle liberally with icing sugar. With a pointed knife *held flat*, lightly score through the almond mixture, starting in the centre and marking the cake into 12 sections. Slide the foil and cake on to the baking sheet and bake for 15 minutes until risen, increase the heat to 220°C, 425°F, Gas 7, and bake for 10 minutes more until the cake rises in a golden mound, reduce the heat again to 200°C, 400°F, Gas 6 and finish cooking for a further 10 to 25 minutes until the bottom crust is baked. Allow to cool on a wire rack and dust with icing sugar before serving.

This cake should be served fresh, the day it is made.

Wedding cake is not part of the French wedding ceremony, but in the villages of Sanxay (Vienne) no wedding is celebrated without a *macaroné* being served.

Le macaroné
(Almond Wedding Pastry)
Makes 20 pieces

pâte sucrée (see page 161)
salt
3 medium sized egg whites
100 g (4 oz) blanched almonds
100 g (4 oz) castor sugar

Line a Swiss roll tin with foil and butter it lightly. Roll out the pastry thinly on a floured greaseproof paper. Put the tin, foil-side down, on the pastry, slide the right hand under the paper and reverse the pastry quickly on to the tin. Press lightly down into the corners, trim the edges, prick the bottom with a fork and set aside. Add a pinch of salt to the egg whites, beat until stiff and set aside.

Heat the oven to 180°C, 350°F, Gas 4.

Chop the almonds finely (do not grind) and mix with the sugar. Beat the egg whites again until stiff and fold the sugar mixture into them with an up-and-over movement. Spread the mixture evenly over the pastry and bake for 15 minutes. Reduce the heat to 170°C, 325°F, Gas 3, and bake for a further 20 minutes until crisp and golden on top. Leave to cool for 5 minutes, cut into half down the centre and across into 2.5 cm (1 inch) wide strips. Remove from the tin and cool on a wire rack.

This cake is at its best when freshly made, but it can be stored for several days if placed in an airtight tin.

Chapter Eleven

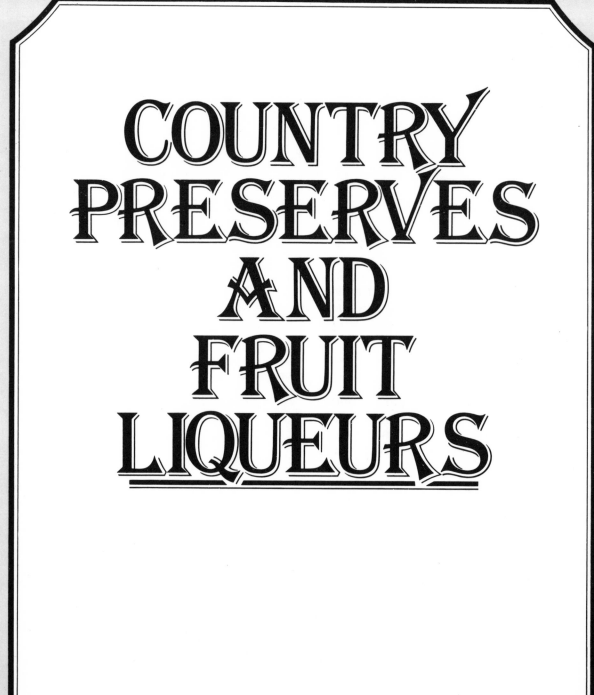

COUNTRY PRESERVES AND FRUIT LIQUEURS

166

Country Preserves

Green tomatoes, windfall apples, small bunches of grapes all go to make some of the most delicious and unusual preserves that fill the French farmhouse storecupboard. In fact, any fruit that cannot be sent to market the country woman makes into jams, jellies or fruit liqueurs.

Confiture de tomates vertes
(Green Tomato Jam)

2.5 kg (5 lb) green tomatoes
2 kg (4 lb) sugar
1 large thin-skinned lemon
½ vanilla pod
4 tablespoons rum

Wash the tomatoes and dry thoroughly. Remove the stem core with an apple corer and cut the fruit into slices just under 5 mm (¼ inch) thick. Layer the tomatoes and sugar in a large earthenware bowl ending with a layer of sugar. Cover and leave overnight in a cool place but do not refrigerate.

Wash and dry the lemon, remove a thick slice from each end and slice the rest, on a plate, into paper-thin slices. Remove the pips, halve the slices and add them, with the juice, to the tomatoes. Stir thoroughly and pour fruit, juice and sugar into the preserving pan. Add the ½ vanilla pod slit down the length. Put the pan over low heat and bring very slowly to boiling point. When simmering, increase the heat and simmer faster for 30 minutes. Increase the heat again slightly and boil fast for 10 minutes. The jam should now be a golden green colour. Stir in the rum.

Test by pouring a little on to a cold plate and leave to cool. When cooked it should wrinkle when pushed with the finger; or when a fingertip is dipped in and slowly raised, the cooked jam should form a thread between finger and plate.

Allow the jam to cool for 5 minutes. Pour into small heated jars and leave to cool completely before sealing first with waxed discs dipped in brandy or sherry, and then with jam covers.

Store in a cool dark place.

All jams and jellies set more easily when small jars are used in preference to large ones.

The mixture of apples used to make the following preserve often includes crab apples, which give the jelly a deep pink tint. When these are not available, dessert apples with bright red peel will help to give a good colour.

Gelée de pommes
(Apple Jelly)

windfall apples
sugar
water

Wash the apples quickly in several changes of cold water. Do not let them soak. Remove all bruised parts and cut the fruit into chunks, peel and core included. Put into the preserving pan, cover with cold water and set over low heat. When simmering, increase the heat slightly and simmer steadily until the fruit and water form a soft mass. Pour into a jelly bag and leave to drip overnight. Do not squeeze the bag or the jelly will be cloudy. Place the jars in a warm oven to heat.

Measure the juice and measure an equal quantity of sugar, cupful for cupful. Put the sugar into the preserving pan, pour the juice over it, and stir thoroughly for 5 minutes. Place over low heat and bring slowly to boiling point, stirring frequently. When simmering and a white crust has formed on top, remove the crust with a slotted spoon, increase the heat and boil fast for 15 minutes. Make sure the sugar has dissolved beforehand. Remove any further crust and test as advised on page 167. Allow to cool for 5 minutes and pour into very hot jars. Leave until cold and seal with waxed discs dipped in brandy or sherry and then with jam covers.

Store in a cool dark place.

Raisiné, the deceptively simple jam made from fresh grape juice, was a great favourite of parsimonious country people in the days when sugar was an expensive commodity, because it is made without. The grapes, however, must be very ripe and sweet (like the small black ones are), as the setting of the jam depends on the natural sugar content of the fruit.

Raisiné
(Grape Jelly)

Take as many ripe black grapes as can be spared from wine-making and strip them from the stalk with a fork into a large earthenware bowl. Crush thoroughly with the bottom of a bottle and pour the mass into a jelly bag. Hang this up over a plastic or earthenware bowl and leave to drip overnight.

Pour the juice into a preserving pan, place over medium heat, and bring to boiling point, skimming off the froth as it rises. Boil steadily until reduced by half, stirring occasionally with a wooden spoon. When reduced, the jam will be thick. Test as advised on page 167.

Stir thoroughly and pour boiling hot into heated jars. Leave to cool, and seal the following day, first with waxed discs dipped in brandy or sherry and then with jam covers.

Store in a cool dark place.

In Provence *raisiné* is given more interest by the addition of sliced apples and pears.

Raisiné composé du Midi
(Grape Jelly with Apples and Pears)

For 2.5 litres (4 pints) grape juice allow 225 g (8 oz) sweet dessert apples, preferably Cox's, and the same quantity of sweet ripe William or Conference pears. It is essential that both should be ripe and tender. Peel the fruit and cut each one into 8 sections. When the *raisiné* has reduced by almost half, add the fruit and cook until soft, stirring frequently with a wooden spatula to prevent the fruit sticking to the bottom of the pan. Test as for the plain *raisiné* and leave to cool for 5 minutes. Stir thoroughly each time before pouring into heated jars. This will prevent the fruit sinking when cold.

Leave to cool, and seal the following day first with waxed discs dipped in brandy or sherry and then with jam covers.

Store in a cool dark place.

Fruit Liqueurs

The fruit liqueurs made in French country people's homes are served with coffee in small quantity. They are less innocuous than they would seem.

The alcoholic content is supplied either by *eau-de-vie*, otherwise known as *alcool à fruits*, and sold by every village grocer in France, or by wine, or wine fortified by an addition of *eau-de-vie*. In the last instance, the *eau-de-vie* can be replaced by brandy. Sometimes the alcohol is simply produced by the fermentation of fruit juice and sugar.

The longer these cordials and liqueurs are left to mature before drinking, the better they will be.

Cerises à l'eau-de-vie
(Morello Cherry Liqueur)

about 1 kg (2 lb) ripe morello cherries
350 g (12 oz) castor sugar
1 litre (1¾ pints) alcohol 80°

Wash and dry the cherries, discard any that are bruised and cut down the stalk to 1 cm (½ inch). Pierce each cherry with a darning needle in two places and put into a wide-topped glass jar, layering the fruit and sugar until the jar is almost full. Fill up with alcohol, cork tightly, seal with wax and leave on a sunny window sill for 2 months, turning and shaking the jar carefully from time to time. Serve in small wine glasses, 3 or 4 cherries for each person just covered with liqueur.

If morello cherries are not available, large black cherries can be preserved by another method. This produces a sweeter liqueur of greater density.

Ratafia de cerises
(Black Cherry Liqueur)

about 1.5 kg (3 lb) black cherries
1 litre (1¾ pints) alcohol 80°
1 stick of cinnamon
3 or 4 grains coriander
350 g (12 oz) castor sugar

Weigh 500 g (1 lb) cherries, wash and dry them, discard any that are bruised, and re-move the stalks. Stone half of them, crush the stones, put them into a large earthenware crock and add the fruit. Crush it all with the end of a bottle, add the alcohol, cinnamon and coriander, cover and leave to infuse for 15 days at room temperature. Wash and dry another 1 kg (2 lb) cherries and cut the stalks down to 1 cm (½ inch). Place them in layers with the sugar in a wide topped glass jar.

Strain the contents of the crock through a piece of old linen into a bowl and pour this liquid over the cherries to fill the jar. Cork tightly, seal and leave to infuse for at least 2 months before serving.

Ratafia aux quatre fruits
(Four Fruit Liqueur)

1 kg (2 lb) black cherries
1 kg (2 lb) ripe raspberries
1 kg (2 lb) redcurrants
450 g (1 lb) blackberries (if available)
alcohol 80°
castor sugar
1 stick of cinnamon

Pick over the fruit and discard any that is bruised or discoloured. Prepare the cherries as advised in the previous recipe with half of the stones crushed. Place fruit and stones in a large earthenware crock and add the rasp-berries, redcurrants and blackberries. Crush it all with the end of a bottle, cover and leave for 3 days. Strain through a piece of old linen into another earthenware crock. Measure the juice and for every litre (1¾ pints), add an equal volume of alcohol 80° and 150 g (5 oz) sugar. Stir well, add stick of cinnamon, cover and leave to infuse for 6 weeks. Filter through filter papers into bottles, cork, seal and allow to mature for at least 2 months before use.

Liqueur de fraises
(Strawberry Liqueur)

250 g (9 oz) ripe strawberries (or raspberries)
1 litre (1¾ pints) *rosé* wine
225 g (8 oz) castor sugar
300 ml (½ pint) alcohol 80° or brandy

Pick over the fruit, removing stalks, and place in a large earthenware jar. Pour in the wine, cover and leave to infuse for 2 days. Pour the wine and fruit into a stainless steel or lined pan, stir in the sugar, place over very low heat and stirring constantly heat very gently, just enough to finish dissolving the sugar. Do not allow to approach boiling point.

Allow to cool completely, strain through a fine sieve, then filter the liquid through filter paper, add the alcohol, stir well and bottle. Cork tightly and store in a cool dry place for at least 2 months before use.

Index